Cloud Analytics with Microsoft Azure

Build modern data warehouses with the combined power of analytics and Azure

Has Altaiar

Jack Lee

Michael Peña

Cloud Analytics with Microsoft Azure

Authors: Has Altaiar, Jack Lee, and Michael Peña

Technical Reviewers: Aram Golbaghikoukia and Aaditya Pokkunuri

Managing Editor: Aditya Datar

Acquisitions Editor: Alicia Wooding

Production Editor: Deepak Chavan

Editorial Board: Sonali Anubhavne, Vishal Bodwani, Ewan Buckingham, Megan Carlisle, Alex Mazonowicz, and Jonathan Wray

First Published: November 2019

Production Reference: 1221119

ISBN: 978-1-83921-640-4

Published by Packt Publishing Ltd.

Livery Place, 35 Livery Street

Birmingham B3 2PB, UK

Table of Contents

Chapter 3: Processing and Visualizing Data   87

Chapter 6: Conclusion 211

Preface

About

This section briefly introduces the author, the coverage of this course, the technical skills you'll need to get started, and the hardware and software requirements required to complete all of the included activities and exercises.

About Cloud Analytics with Microsoft Azure

With data being generated at an exponential speed, organizations all over the world are migrating their infrastructure to the cloud. Application management becomes much easier when you use a cloud platform to build, manage, and deploy your services and applications.

Cloud Analytics with Microsoft Azure covers all that you need to extract useful insights from your data. You'll explore the power of data with big data analytics, the Internet of Things (IoT), machine learning, artificial intelligence, and DataOps. You'll also delve into data analytics by studying use cases that focus on creating actionable insights from near-real-time data. As you advance, you'll learn to build an end-to-end analytics pipeline on the cloud with machine learning and deep learning concepts.

By the end of this book, you'll have developed a solid understanding of data analytics with Azure and its practical implementation.

About the Authors

Has Altaiar is a software engineer at heart and a consultant by trade. Has lives in Melbourne, Australia, and is the Executive Director at vNEXT Solutions. His work focuses on data, IoT, and AI on Microsoft Azure, and two of his latest IoT projects won multiple awards. Has is also a Microsoft Azure MVP and a regular organizer and speaker at local and international conferences, including Microsoft Ignite, NDC, and ServerlessDays. He's also a board member of the Global AI Community. You can follow him on Twitter at **@hasaltaiar**.

Jack Lee is a senior Azure certified consultant and an Azure practice lead with a passion for software development, cloud, and DevOps innovations. He is an active Microsoft tech community contributor and has presented at various user groups and conferences, including the Global Azure Bootcamp at Microsoft Canada. Jack is an experienced mentor and judge at Hackathons and is also the president of a user group that focuses on Azure, DevOps, and software development. Jack has been recognized as a Microsoft MVP for his contributions to the tech community. You can follow Jack on Twitter at **@jlee_consulting**.

Michael Peña is an experienced technical consultant based in Sydney, Australia. He is a Microsoft MVP and a certified professional with over 10 years of experience in data, mobile, cloud, web, and DevOps. Throughout these years, he wore various hats but considered himself a developer at heart. He is also an international speaker, having spoken at numerous events, including the Microsoft Ignite, NDC, DDD, Cross-Platform Summit, and various in-person and virtual meet-ups. Michael has interned with Microsoft and is also a Microsoft student partner alumnus. You can follow him on Twitter at **@mjtpena**.

Learning Objectives

By the end of this course, you will be able to:

- Explore the concepts of modern data warehouses and data pipelines
- Discover different design considerations while applying a cloud analytics solution
- Design an end-to-end analytics pipeline on the cloud
- Differentiate between structured, semi-structured, and unstructured data
- Choose a cloud-based service for your data analytics solutions
- Use Azure services to ingest, store and analyze data of any scale

Audience

If you're planning to adopt the cloud analytics model for your business, this book will help you understand the design and business considerations that you must keep in mind. Though not necessary, a basic understanding of data analytics concepts such as data streaming, data types, the machine learning life cycle, and Docker containers will help you get the most out of the book.

Approach

Cloud Analytics with Microsoft Azure explains complex concepts in an easy-to-understand manner. Also, the book contains several quick-start guides to cover major concepts with hands-on experience.

Hardware Requirements

For the optimal student experience, we recommend the following hardware configuration:

- Processor: Intel Core i5 or equivalent
- Memory (RAM): At least 1 GB available, 1.5 GB or more recommended
- Display: At least 1440x900 or 1600x900 (16:9) recommended
- CPU: 1 gigahertz (GHz) or faster x86- or x64-bit processor recommended

Software Requirements

We also recommend that you have the following softwares installed in advance:

- Windows 7 / Windows Server 2008 R2, or later
- .NET 4.5
- Internet Explorer 10 or later

Conventions

Code words in the text, database table names, folder names, filenames, file extensions, pathnames, dummy URLs, user input, and Twitter handles are shown as follows:

"The following code snippet creates a table called **TweetsStream** in the Azure Synapse Analytics to receive the stream. This table has two simple columns—one for the **timestamp** and one for the Value that is received from the data stream. The example below assigns **ROUND_ROBIN** as the distribution policy for this table"

A block of code is set as follows:

```
CREATE TABLE [dbo].[TweetsStream]
(
  [timestamp] DATETIME NULL,
  [Value] BIGINT NULL
)
WITH
(
  DISTRIBUTION = ROUND_ROBIN,
  CLUSTERED INDEX ([timestamp])
)
```

Installation and Setup

You can install Power BI desktop (https://packt.live/37hUTmK) and start creating interactive reports.

Start your cloud analytics journey by signing up at https://packt.live/2Xqtj22.

1

Introducing Analytics on Azure

According to a survey by Dresner Advisory Service in 2019, an all-time high of 48% of organizations say business intelligence on the cloud is either critical or very important in conducting their business operations. *Cloud Computing and Business Intelligence Market Study* also showed that sales and marketing teams get the most value out of analytics.

As businesses grow, they generate massive amounts of data every day. This data comes from different sources such as mobile phones, the **Internet of Things** (**IoT**) sensors, and various **Software-as-a-Service** (**SAAS**) products such as **Customer Relationship Managers** (**CRMs**). Enterprises and businesses need to scale and modernize their data architecture and infrastructure in order to cope with the demand to stay competitive in their respective industries.

Having cloud-scale analytics capability is the go-to strategy for achieving this growth. Instead of managing your own data center, harnessing the power of the cloud allows your businesses to be more accessible to your users. With the help of a cloud service provider such as Microsoft Azure, you can accelerate your data analytics practice without the limitations of your IT infrastructure. The game has changed in terms of maintaining IT infrastructures, as **data lakes** and the cloud data warehouse are capable of storing and maintaining massive amounts of data.

Simply gathering data does not add value to your business; you need to derive insights from it and help your business grow using data analytics. Azure is more than just a hub for gathering data; it is an invaluable resource for data analytics. Data analytics provides you with the ability to understand your business and customers better. By applying various data science concepts, such as machine learning, regression analysis, classification algorithms, and time series forecasting, you can test your hypotheses and make data-driven decisions for the future. However, one of the challenges that organizations continuously face is how to derive these analytical modeling capabilities quickly when processing billions of data rows. This is where having a modern data warehouse and data pipeline can help (more on this in the next sections).

There are a number of ways by which data analytics can help your business thrive. In the case of retail, if you understand your customers better, you will have a better idea of what products you should sell, where to sell them, when to sell them, and how to sell them. In the financial sector, data analytics is helping fight crimes by detecting fraudulent transactions and providing more informed risk assessments based on historical criminal intelligence.

This chapter will cover fundamental topics on the power of data with **big data analytics**, **IoT**, **Machine Learning** (**ML**) and **Artificial Intelligence** (**AI**), and **DataOps**. You will also learn why Microsoft Azure is the platform of choice for performing analytics on cloud. Lastly, you will study the fundamental concepts of a modern data warehouse and data pipelines.

The Power of Data

As a consumer, you have seen how the advent of data has influenced our activities in the daily grind. Most popular entertainment applications, such as YouTube, now provide a customized user experience with features such as video recommendations based on our interests and search history logging information. It is now child's play to discover new content that's similar to our preferred content and also to find new and popular trending content.

Due to the major shift in wearable technology, it has also become possible to keep track of our health statistics by monitoring heart rates, blood pressure, and so on. These devices then formulate a tailored recommendation based on the averages of these statistics. But these personalized health stats are only a sample of the massive data collection happening every day on a global scale–in which we actively contribute.

Millions of people all over the world use social networking platforms and search engines every day. Internet giants like Facebook, Instagram, and Google use clickstream data to come up with new innovations and improve their services.

Data collection is also carried out on an extensive level under projects such as *The Great Elephant Census*, *eBird* that aim to boost wildlife conversation. Data driven techniques have even been adopted for tiger conservation projects in India.

It even plays an invaluable role in global efforts to compile evidence, causes, and possible responses to climate change–to understand sea surface temperature, analyze natural calamities such as coastal flooding, and global warming patterns in a collective effort to save the ecosystem.

Organizations like Global Open Data for Agriculture and Nutrition (GODAN), which can be used farmers, ranchers, and consumers alike, contribute to this tireless data collection as well.

Furthermore (as with the advent of wearable technology), data analysis is contributing to pioneering advancements in the healthcare sector. Patient datasets are analyzed to identify patterns and early symptoms of diseases in order to divine better solutions to known problems.

The scale of data being talked about here is massive–hence, the popular term "big data" is used to describe the harnessing power of this data at scale.

Note

You can read more about this here.

Big Data Analytics

The term big data is often used to describe massive volumes of data that traditional tools cannot handle. It can be characterized with five Vs:

- **Volume**: This indicates the volume of data that needs to be analyzed for big data analytics. We are now dealing with larger datasets than ever before. This has been made possible because of the availability of electronic products such as mobile devices and IoT sensors that have been widely adopted all over the globe for commercial purposes.

- **Velocity**: This refers to the rate at which data is being generated. Devices and platforms, such as those just mentioned, constantly produce data on a large scale and at rapid speed. This makes collecting, processing, analyzing, and serving data at rapid speeds necessary.

- **Variety**: This refers to the structure of data being produced. Data sources are inconsistent. Some are structured and some are unstructured. (You will learn more about this in the following pages.)

- **Value**: This refers to the value of the data being extracted. Accessible data may not always be valuable. With the right tools, you can derive value from the data in a cost-effective and scalable way.

- **Veracity**: This is the quality or trustworthiness of data. A raw dataset will usually contain a lot of __noise__ and __bias__ and will need cleaning. Having a large dataset is not useful if most of the data is not accurate.

Big data analytics is the process of finding patterns, trends, and correlations in unstructured data to derive meaningful insights that shape business decisions. This unstructured data is usually large in file size (images, videos, and social graphs, for instance).

This does not mean that relational databases are not relevant for big data. In fact, modern data warehouse platforms like Azure Synapse Analytics (formerly known as Azure SQL Data Warehouse) support structured and semi-structured data (such as JSON) and can infinitely scale to support terabytes to petabytes of data. Using Microsoft Azure, you have the flexibility to choose any platform. These technologies can complement each other to achieve a robust data analytics pipeline.

Here are some of the best use cases of big data analytics:

- **Social media analysis**: Through social media sites such as Twitter, Facebook, and Instagram, companies can learn what customers are saying about their products and services. Social media analysis helps companies to target their audiences depending on user preferences and market trends. The challenges here are the massive amount of data and the unstructured nature of tweets and posts.

- **Fraud prevention**: This is one of the most familiar use cases of big data. One of the prominent features of big data analytics when used for fraud prevention is the ability to detect anomalies in a dataset. Validating credit card transactions by understanding transaction patterns such as location data and categories of purchased items is an example of this. The biggest challenge here is ensuring that the AI/ML models are clean and unbiased. There might be a chance that the model was trained just for a specific parameter such as user's country of origin, hence the model will focus on determining patterns on just user's location and might miss out on other parameters.

- **Price optimization**: Using big data analytics, you can predict what price points will yield the best results based on historical market data. This allows companies to ensure that they do not price their items too high or too low. The challenge here is that there are many factors that can affect prices. Focusing on just a specific factor such as competitor's price might eventually train your model to just focus on that area, and may disregard other factors such as weather and traffic data.

Big data for businesses and enterprises is usually accompanied by the concept of having an IoT infrastructure, where hundreds, thousands, or even millions of devices are connected to a network that constantly sends data to a server.

Internet of Things (IoT)

IoT plays a vital role in scaling your application to go beyond your current data sources. IoT is simply an interconnection of devices that are embedded to serve a single purpose in objects around us to send and receive data. IoT allows us to constantly gather more data about "things" without manually encoding them into a database.

A smartwatch is a good example of an IoT device that constantly measures your body's vital measurements. Instead of getting a measuring device and encoding it to a system, a smartwatch allows you to record your data automatically. Another good example is a device tracker for an asset which captures location, temperature, and humidity information. This allows logistics companies to monitor their items in transit, ensuring the quality and efficiency of their services.

At scale, these IoT devices generate anywhere from gigabytes to terabytes of data. This data is usually stored in a data lake in a raw, unstructured format, and is later analyzed to derive business insights. A data lake is a centralized repository of all structured, semi-structured, and unstructured data. In the example of the logistic company mentioned above, patterns (such as the best delivery routes) could be generated. The data could also be used to understand anomalies such as data leakage or suspected fraudulent activities.

Machine Learning and Artificial Intelligence

As your data grows in size, it opens a lot of opportunities for businesses to go beyond understanding business trends and patterns. Machine learning and artificial intelligence are examples of innovations that you can exploit with your data. Building your artificial intelligence and machine learning capability is relatively easy now because of the availability of technologies and the ability to scale your storage and compute on the cloud.

ML and AI are terms that are often mixed together. In a nutshell, machine learning is a subset (or application) of artificial intelligence. Machine learning aims to allow systems to learn from past datasets and adapt automatically without human assistance. This is made possible by a series of algorithms being applied to the dataset; the algorithm analyzes the data in near-real time and then comes up with possible actions based on accuracy or confidence derived from previous experience.

The word 'learning' indicates that the program is constantly learning from the data fed to it. The aim of machine learning is to strive for accuracy rather than success. There are two main categories of machine learning algorithms: **supervised** and **unsupervised**.

Supervised machine learning algorithms create a mapping function to map the input variables with the output variable. The algorithm uses the existing datasets to train itself for predicting the output. Classification is a form of supervised ML that can be used in applications such as image categorization or customer segmentation, which is used for targeted marketing campaigns.

Unsupervised machine learning, on the other hand, is when you let the program find a pattern of its own without any labels. A good example is understanding customer purchase patterns when buying products. You get inherent groupings (**clustering**) according to purchasing behaviors, and the program can associate customers and products according to patterns of purchase. For instance, you may discern that customers who buy Product A tend to buy Product B too. This is an example of a user-based recommendation algorithm and market-based analysis. What it would eventually mean for users is that when they buy a particular item, such as a book, the user is also encouraged to buy other books that belong to the same series, genre, or category.

Artificial intelligence extends beyond what machine learning can do. It is about making decisions and aiming for success rather than accuracy. One way to think of it is that machine learning aims to gain knowledge while artificial intelligence aims for wisdom or intelligence. An example of AI in action would be Boston Dynamic's Atlas robot, which can navigate freely in the open world and avoid obstacles without the aid of human control. The robot does not fully depend on the historical map data to navigate. However, for machine learning, it's about creating or predicting a pattern from historical data analysis. Similar to the robot's navigation, it is about understanding the most optimal route by creating patterns based from historical and crowd-sourced traffic data.

Setting up a modern data warehouse with cloud analytics is the key factor in preparing to execute ML/AI. Without migrating the workloads to the cloud, deriving ML/AI models will encounter various roadblocks in order to maximize the business value of these emerging technologies. A modern data warehouse and analytics pipeline are the backbone that enables these.

Microsoft is a leader in machine learning and artificial intelligence as they have been driving a lot of innovation throughout their products and tools—for instance, Window's digital assistant, Cortana, and Office 365's live captions and subtitles. They offer a range of products, tools, and services such as Microsoft Cognitive Services, ML Studio, Azure Machine Learning Service and ML.NET.

Microsoft is setting an example with their initiative *AI for Good*, which aims to make the world more sustainable and accessible through AI. One interesting project in particular is *AI for Snow Leopards*, in which Microsoft uses AI technology to detect snow leopards (who are almost invisible in snow) in order to protect the endangered species.

Exploring artificial intelligence and deep learning specifically the data science and formula aspects are not the focus of this book, but you will tackle some concepts once in a while in later chapters (see more on this in *Chapter 3, Processing and Visualizing Data*).

DataOps

In order to be efficient and agile with implementing data analytics in your company, you need the right culture and processes. This is where the concept of **DataOps** comes in. DataOps removes the co-ordination barrier between data (analysts, engineers, and scientists) and operations (administrators and operations managers) teams in order to achieve speed and accuracy in data analytics.

DataOps is about a culture of collaboration between different roles and functions. Data scientists have access to real-time data to explore, prepare, and serve. Automated processes and flows prove invaluable to this collaborative effort between analysts and developers, as it provides easy access to this data through visualization tools. Relevant data should be served to end users via web or mobile applications; this is usually possible with a use of **Application Programming Interface** (**API**). For CEOs, DataOps means faster decision-making, as it allows them to monitor their business at a high level without waiting for team leaders to report. The following figure tries to explain the idea of a collaborative DataOps culture:

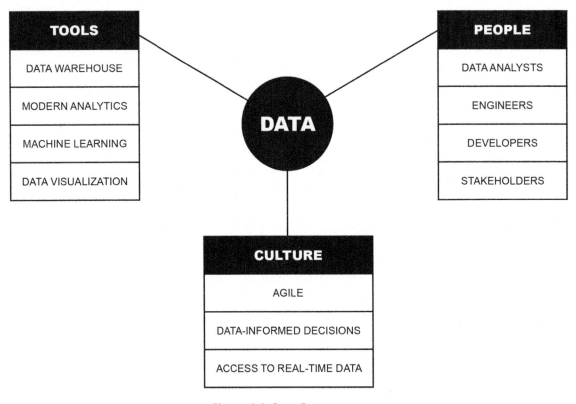

Figure 1.1: DataOps process

Once a team attains the desired speed and accuracy in testing their hypotheses (such as the likelihood of someone buying a product based on her/his characteristics and behavior), they are able to derive better insights. Once there are better insights, there are more actionable and reasonable decision points for business stakeholders that minimize risks and maximize profits.

Why Microsoft Azure?

Microsoft Azure is an enterprise-grade set of cloud computing services created by Microsoft using their own managed data centers. Azure is the only cloud with a true end-to-end analytics solution. With Azure, analysts can derive insights in seconds from all enterprise data. Azure provides a mature and robust data flow without limitations on concurrency.

Azure supports **Infrastructure as a Service** (**IAAS**), **Platform as a Service** (**PAAS**), and **SAAS**. Many government institutions across the world as well as 95% of Fortune 500 companies use Azure, ranging from industries such as healthcare and financial services to retail, and manufacturing.

Microsoft is a technology conglomerate that has empowered many people to achieve more with less, for decades, with their software, tools, and platforms. Azure provides flexibility. Familiar Microsoft tools and infrastructures (such as SQL Server, Windows Server, **Internet Information Services** (**IIS**), and .NET) or tools such as MySQL, Linux, PHP, Python, Java, or any other open source technologies can all run on the Azure cloud. Gone are the days when you could only work on a walled-garden set of tools and technologies.

Azure provides you with various products and services, depending on your needs. You have the option of doing everything in a bespoke way, from managing your IAAS by spinning up Windows Server virtual machines with Enterprise SQL Server installed, to using a managed PAAS offering such as Azure Synapse Analytics (more on this in *Chapter 2, Building Your Modern Data Warehouse*).

The following figure shows the wide range of data-specific Azure tools and services that can be used to create end-to-end data pipelines:

Figure 1.2: Microsoft Azure data-related services

Azure grants you the flexibility to choose the best approach to solve a problem for yourself, rather than be forced to bend a less adaptable product to perform an unnatural function. You're not just limited to SQL Server, either. You also have the flexibility to choose other types of databases or storage, whether through a service installed on a Linux server or containerized solution, or a managed platform (such as Azure Cosmos DB for your Cassandra and MongoDB instances). This is very important because, in the real world, different scenarios require different solutions, tools, and products.

Microsoft Azure provides you with an end-to-end platform, from Azure Active Directory for managing your user identity and access, to Azure IoT offerings (such as IoT Hub) for gathering data from hundreds and thousands of IoT devices. It also provides services such as development tools and cloud hosting options for getting your developers up to speed, as well as various analytics and machine learning tools which enable data scientists, data engineers, and data analysts to be more productive (more on this in *Chapter 3, Processing and Visualizing Data*).

The full spectrum of Azure services is too wide to cover here, so instead, this book will focus on the key data warehousing and business intelligence suite of products: Azure Data Factory, Azure Data Lake, Azure Synapse Analytics, Azure Databricks, Azure Analysis Services, Power BI, and Azure Machine Learning (refer to *Chapter 2, Building Your Modern Data Warehouse*, and *Chapter 3, Processing and Visualizing Data*).

Security

Microsoft views security as the top priority. When it comes to data, privacy and security are non-negotiable; there will always be threats. Azure has the most advanced security and privacy features in the analytics space. Azure services support data protection through **Virtual Networks** (**VNets**) so that, even though they are in the cloud, data points cannot be accessed by the public internet. Only the users in the same VNet can communicate with each other. For web applications, you get a **Web Application Firewall** (**WAF**) provided by Azure Application Gateway, which ensures that only valid requests can get into your network.

With role-based access control (**authorization**), you can ensure that only those with the right roles, such as administrators, have access to specific components and the capabilities of different resources. **Authentication**, on the other hand, ensures that if you don't have the right credentials (such as passwords), you will not able to access a resource. Authorization and authentication are built into various services and components of Microsoft Azure with the help of Azure Active Directory.

Azure also provides a service called **Azure Key Vault**. Key Vault allows you to safely store and manage secrets and passwords, create encryption keys, and manage certificates so that applications do not have direct access to private keys. By following this pattern with Key Vault, you do not have to hardcode your secrets and passwords in your source code and script repository.

Azure Synapse Analytics uses ML and AI to protect your data. In Azure SQL, Microsoft provides advanced data security to ensure that your data is protected. This includes understanding if your database has vulnerabilities, such as port numbers, that are publicly available. These capabilities also allow you to be more compliant to various standards, such as **GDPR** (**General Data Protection Regulation**), by ensuring that customer data that are considered sensitive are classified. Azure SQL also recently announced their new features, **row-level security** (**RLS**) and **column-level security** (**CLS**), to control access to rows and columns in a database table, based on the user characteristics.

Microsoft invests at least 1 billion dollars each year in the cybersecurity space, including the Azure platform. Azure holds various credentials and awards from independent assessment bodies, which ensures that you can trust Azure in all security aspects, from physical security (such that no unauthorized users can get physical access to data centers) to application-level security.

These are a few security features that you need to consider if you are maintaining your own data center.

Cloud Scale

Azure changed the industry by making data analytics cost-efficient. Before the mass adoption of cloud computing, in order to plan for data analytics with terabytes, or even petabytes, of data, you needed to properly plan things and ensure that you had the capital expenditure to do it. This would mean a very high upfront infrastructure and professional services costs, just to get started. But, with Azure, you can start small (many of the services have free tiers). You can scale your cloud resources effortlessly up or down, in or out, within minutes. Azure has democratized scaling capability by making it economically viable and accessible for everyone, as shown in *Figure 1.3*:

Figure 1.3: Microsoft Azure regions

Microsoft Azure currently has 54 regions supporting 140 countries. Some enterprises and business industries require that your data is hosted within the same country as business operations. With the availability of different data centers worldwide, it is easy for you to expand to other regions. This multi-region approach is also beneficial in terms of making your applications highly available.

The true power of the cloud is its elasticity. This allows you to not only scale resources up, but also scale them down when necessary. In data science, this is very useful because data science entails variable workloads. When data scientists and engineers are analyzing a dataset, for instance, there is a need for more computation. Azure, through Databricks (more on this in *Chapter 2, Building Your Modern Data Warehouse*), allows you to scale according to demand. Then, during off-peak times (such as 7 PM to 7 AM on weekdays and weekends), when the scientists and engineers don't need the processing power to analyze data, you can scale down your resources so that you don't have to pay for running resources 24/7. Databricks basically offers a "pay-as-you-go" or "pay-what-you-use" service.

Azure also provides a **Service Level Agreement** (**SLA**) for their services as their commitments to ensure uptime and connectivity for their production customers. If downtime or an incident occurs, they will apply service credits (rebates) to the resources that were affected. This will give you peace of mind as your application will always be available with a minimal amount of downtime.

There are different scaling approaches and patterns that Microsoft Azure provides:

- **Vertical scaling**: This is when more resources are added to the same instance (server or service). An example of this is when a virtual machine is scaled up from 4 GB of RAM to 16 GB of RAM. This is a simple and straightforward approach to take when your application needs to scale. However, there is a technical maximum limit on how much an instance can be scaled up, and it is the most expensive scaling approach.

- **Horizontal scaling**: This is when you deploy your application to multiple instances. This would logically mean that you can scale your application infinitely because you don't use a single machine to perform your operations. This flexibility also introduces some complexities. These complexities are usually addressed by performing various patterns and the use of different orchestration technologies, such as Docker and Kubernetes.

- **Geographical scaling**: This is when you scale your applications to different geographical locations for two major reasons: resilience and reduced latency. Resilience allows your application to freely operate in that region without all resources being connected to a master region. Reduced latency would mean users of that region can get their web requests faster because of their proximity to the data center.

- **Sharding**: This is one of the techniques for distributing huge volumes of related, structured data onto multiple independent databases.

- **Development, Testing, Acceptance, and Production** (**DTAP**): This is the approach of having multiple instances living in different logical environments. This is usually done to separate development and test servers from staging and production servers. Azure DevTest Labs offers a development and testing environment that can be configured with group policies.

Another advantage of your business being cloud-scale is the availability of your services. With Azure, it is easier to make your infrastructure and resources geo-redundant—that is, available to multiple regions and data centers across the world. Say you want to expand your business from Australia to Canada. You can achieve that by making your SQL Server **geo-redundant** so that Canadian users do not need to query against the application and database instance in Australia.

Azure, despite being a collective suite of products and service offerings, does not force you to go "all in". This means that you can start by implementing a hybrid architecture of combined on-premises data centers and cloud (Azure). There are different approaches and technologies involved in a hybrid solution, such as using **Virtual Private Networks** (**VPNs**) and Azure ExpressRoute, if you need dedicated access.

With Azure Data Factory (there'll be more on this in *Chapter 2, Building Your Modern Data Warehouse*), Azure allows you to get a snapshot of data sources from your on-premises SQL Server. The same concept applies when you have other data sources from other cloud providers or SAAS products; you have the flexibility to get a copy of that data to your Azure data lake. This flexibility is highly convenient because it does not put you in a **vendor lock-in** position where you need to do a full migration.

Top Business Drivers for Adopting Data Analytics on the Cloud

Different companies have different reasons for adopting data analytics using a public cloud like Microsoft Azure. But more often than not, it boils down to three major reasons: rapid growth and scale, reducing costs, and driving innovation.

Rapid Growth and Scale

Enterprises and businesses need to rapidly expand their digital footprint. With the rapid growth of mobile applications—particularly, media types (such as images and videos), IoT sensors, and social media data—there is just so much data to capture. This means enterprises and businesses need to scale their infrastructure to support these massive demands. Company database sizes continuously grow from gigabytes of data to terabytes, or even petabytes, of data.

End users are more demanding now than ever. If your application does not respond within seconds, the user is more likely to disengage with your service or product.

Scaling does not only apply to the consumers of the applications; it is also important for data scientists, data engineers, and data analysts in order to analyze a company's data. Scaling an infrastructure is vital, as you cannot expect your data engineers to handle massive chunks of data (gigabytes to terabytes) and run scripts for testing your data models on a single machine. Even if you do serve this in a single high-performance server instance, it's going to take weeks or days for it to finish the test. Not to mention the fact that it's going to cause performance bottlenecks for the end users who are consuming the same database.

With a modern data warehouse like Azure Synapse Analytics, you have some managed capabilities to scale, such as a dedicated caching layer. Caching will allow analysts, engineers, and scientists to query faster.

Reducing Costs

Due to scaling demands, enterprises and businesses need to have a mechanism to expand their data infrastructure in a cost-effective and financially viable way. It is too expensive to set up a data warehouse on premises. The following are just a few of the cost considerations:

- The waiting time for server delivery and associated internal procurement processes
- Networking and other physical infrastructure costs, such as hardware-cooling and data center real estate
- Professional services costs associated with setting up and maintaining these servers
- Licensing costs (if any)
- The productivity lost from people and teams who cannot ship their products faster

With a modern data warehouse, you can spin up new high-performance servers with high-performance graphics cards on demand. And with the use of a cloud provider such as Microsoft Azure, you will only need to pay for the time that you use these servers. You can shut them down if you don't need them anymore. Not only can you turn them off on demand, but if it turns out that a particular service is not suitable to your requirements, you can delete these resources and just provision a different service.

Azure also provides a discount for "reserved" instances that you are committing to use for a specific amount of time. These are very helpful for those databases, storage solutions, and applications that need to be up 24/7 with minimal downtime.

Driving Innovation

Companies need to constantly innovate in this very competitive market, otherwise someone else will rise up and take the market share. But obviously, no one can predict the future with 100% accuracy; hence, companies need to have a mechanism to explore new things based on what they know.

One good example of this is the Business Process Outsourcing (BPO) and telecommunications (telco) industries, where there are petabytes of data that may not have been explored yet. With Microsoft Azure's modern data warehouse, actors in such industries can have the infrastructure to do data exploration. With Azure Data Lake, Azure Data Factory, Azure Synapse Analytics, Azure Databricks, Power BI, and Azure Machine Learning, they can explore their data to drive business decisions. Maybe they can come up with a data model that can detect fraudulent actions or better understand their customer preferences and expectations to improve satisfaction ratings. With advanced analytics, these companies can come up with decisions that are relevant today (and possibly in the future) and are not just restricted to analyzing historical data.

What if you want to create an autonomous vehicle? You will need a robust data warehouse to store your datasets and a tremendous amount of data processing. You need to capture massive amounts of data—whether through pictures or videos that the car is continuously capturing—and need to come up with a response almost instantly based on your data set and algorithms.

Using a cloud provider like Microsoft Azure would allow you to test and validate your ideas early on, without a massive investment. With Azure, you can rapidly prototype your ideas and explore possibilities. What if it turns out that the product or service that you or your team is working on does not really gain traction? If you are doing this on-premises, you will still have high liability and operations costs since you physically own the infrastructure, in addition to any associated licensing and services costs.

Why Do You Need a Modern Data Warehouse?

A data warehouse is a centralized repository that aggregates different (often disparate) data sources. The main difference between a data warehouse and a database is that data warehouses are meant for OLAP (Online Analytical Processing) and databases, on the other hand, are intended for OLTP (Online Transaction Processing). OLAP means that data warehouses are primarily used to generate Analytics, Business Intelligence, and even Machine Learning models. OLTP means that databases are primarily used for transactions. These transactions are the day-to-day operations of applications where they concurrently read and write data to databases.

A data warehouse is essential if you want to analyze your big data as it also contains historical data (often called cold data). Most of the data stored has legacy information, such as data stored 5 years ago, 10 years ago, or even 15 years ago. You probably don't want the same database instance that your end users are querying against to also contain that historical data, as it might affect your performance when at scale.

Here are some of the advantages of having a modern data warehouse:

- Supports any data source
- Highly scalable and available
- Provides insights from analytical dashboards in real-time
- Supports a machine learning environment

The various tools and services that constitute the modern data warehouse are connected with each other as follows:

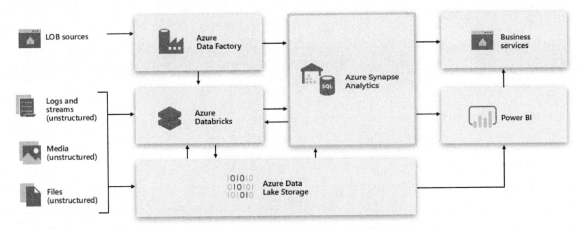

Figure 1.4: Modern Data Warehouse architecture

There are a lot of emerging patterns and architectures for data warehousing, but the most popular ones are those that support separation of duties and responsibilities on different phases of the data pipeline (more on this in the *Creating a Data Pipeline* section).

In order to understand what it means for a data warehouse to be modern; you first need to understand how you create and manage a traditional one. It boils down to two major concepts:

- **Compute**: This refers to the ability to process the data and make sense out of it. It can be in the form of a database query to make the results accessible to another interface, such as web applications.

- **Storage**: This refers to the ability to keep data in order for it to be accessible at any time in the future.

A modern data warehouse separates compute and storage in cost-effective ways. Unlike the case traditionally with SQL Server and **SQL Server Integration Services** (**SSIS**), the pricing model involves both the storage capacity and computing power to analyze data. Azure is the first cloud provider to offer a data warehouse that separates compute and storage.

Another change in pattern is that the traditional **ETL** (**Extract-Transform-Load**) model of data warehousing has now changed to **ELT** (**Extract-Load-Transform**). In the traditional ETL model, analysts are accustomed to waiting for the data to be transformed first, since they don't have direct access to all data sources. In a modern data warehouse, massive amounts of data can be stored to either a data lake or data warehouse, and can be transformed anytime by analysts without the need to wait for data engineers or database admins to serve the data.

Of course, there are more factors to consider in order to modernize your data warehouse, such as extensibility, disaster recovery, and availability. However, this section will focus on compute for the time being.

Bringing Your Data Together

In the past, databases were often the only source of data for your applications. But nowadays, you have hundreds and thousands of different data sources. The data coming from these different sources has different data types—some structured, some unstructured.

Structured Data: The word 'structured' suggests that there is a pattern that can be easily interpreted. This usually comes with a predefined set of models and a schema. A **Relational Database Management System** (**RDBMS**) such as Microsoft SQL Server is a common example of data storage solution that is structured. This is because it comes with a database schema and table columns that define the data that you are storing

Here are some examples of structured data types:

- Customer name(s)
- Address(es)
- Geolocation
- Date and time
- Mobile and phone numbers
- Credit card numbers
- Product names and Stock Keeping Units (SKUs)
- General transaction information such as "From" and "To" with time stamps and amount values

A good example of structured data is the information provided by the users when signing up to an application for the first time. They are presented with a form that needs to be filled. Once that person clicks the submit button, it sends the data to a database and inserts it into a user table with predefined columns: names, addresses, and other details. This will then allow the user to log into the application since the system can now look up the existing record for the registered user in the database.

From there, a user can access the application and perform transactions, such as transferring money and assets. In time, users will generate a series of transactions that will eventually make your database larger. Your database schema will also expand to support different business requirements.

Once you have enough data, you can perform data exploration. This is where you start looking for patterns in data. You may identify fraudulent transactions and test hypotheses by analyzing large and repeated transaction amounts from the same user.

Your data exploration is limited because you can only base it on a dataset that is structured and with semantic form. What if you also want to consider other data sources that are unstructured, such as free-form text? An example is a transaction description, that may state the nature or the recipient of the transaction. You don't want to manually read each transaction description and insert it in the right column of a database table. You probably want to extract only the relevant information and transform it into a structured format. This is where unstructured data comes in.

Unstructured Data: This data type, more or less, is the "the rest"–that is, everything that isn't structured data. This is mainly because you are not limited to anything. Unstructured data types usually don't have a predefined data model that can fit directly to a database. Unstructured data can be "text-heavy" and is usually read per line or is space-separated. Here are some examples of unstructured data sources:

- Image files
- Videos
- Email messages and documents
- Log files
- IoT devices and sensors
- NoSQL databases such as MongoDB
- Social media and Microsoft Graph

Image files and videos are classified as unstructured data because of their dynamic nature. Although their metadata is something you can consider as structured (like title, artist, filename, etc.), the content itself is unstructured. With modern tools and data analytics technology, you can now examine this data and make sense of it. The usual example is face recognition in either images or videos.

Emails, documents, and log files all have metadata, but what you're actually more interested in is the content of those files. Usually, in emails, documents, and log files, data is separated per line and the messages are unstructured. Here you would want to describe the content without manually reading everything (which could be hundreds, or even millions of files). An example is doing sentiment analysis on content to determine whether the prevailing emotion is happy, sad, or angry. For log files, you probably want to separate the error messages, time stamps (dates), and measurements (traces) between messages.

IoT devices and sensors, similarly to log files, are used to capture measurements and errors about a certain item. The main difference is that these devices usually work on a large scale of clusters (hundreds to thousands of devices) and continuously stream data. Data generated from these devices is semi-structured or unstructured since it is in JSON or XML format. Modern technologies, such as Azure IoT services, already solve these complexities with services like Azure IoT Hub, which aggregates all this data from various sensors and continuously exports it to a data source. Sometimes you can classify this data as semi-structured since these traces and logs are things that a system can easily understand.

Social media platforms and Microsoft Graph both provide semi-structured data. It is classified this way because just querying all of Twitter's tweets about a topic is not enough. The results don't really make a lot of sense until you do some analysis of them. The primary focus is to discern patterns and anomalies. For example, you may want to identify trends about news and topics but also want to remove data that is irrelevant, such as tweets coming from fake accounts.

Interestingly, some **Line of Business** (**LOB**) applications provide both structured and unstructured data. For example, both Microsoft Dynamics CRM and Salesforce provide structured data that can easily be interpreted and exported to your SQL database tables, such as data for products and their amounts and value. However, they also support unstructured data such as images, videos, and "note text". Note that, even though "note text" is a string, it can still be considered as unstructured data because it is designed to be "free text". It doesn't have a proper format to follow, but it is still worth exploring. A common scenario for its use is to understand why sales were not successful.

Creating a Data Pipeline

Once you have identified your data sources, the next step is to create a data pipeline (sometimes also referred to as a data flow). At a high level, the steps involved are data ingestion, data storage, data preparation and training, data modeling and serving, and data visualization.

With this approach, you will build a highly scalable architecture that serves all the users of the system: from end users, data engineers and scientists who are doing the data exploration, and analysts who interpret the data for the business, to even the CEO if she/he wants to see what's happening with the business in real time:

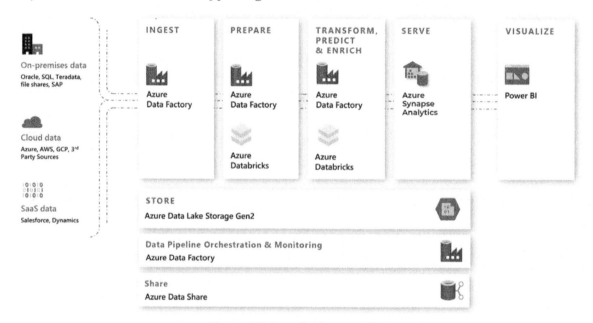

Figure 1.5: Sample data pipeline

Data Ingestion

Data ingestion means transferring data (structured and unstructured) from the source to your storage, data lake, or data warehouse.

This would involve something such as Azure Data Factory (more on this in *Chapter 2, Building Your Modern Data Warehouse*) transferring data from various sources such as on-premises databases and SAAS products to a data lake. This step allows you to manage your **Extract- Transform-Load** (**ETL**) and **Extract-Load-Transform** (**ELT**) workflows without the need for manual reconciliation.

This is not a one-time process. Ideally, this is something you schedule or set to be triggered so that your data lake gets a historical snapshot from time to time. An example of this is a connection from your CRM tools, such as Microsoft Dynamics CRM, to Azure Data Lake by means of Azure Data Factory. This will allow data scientists and data engineers to explore this data at different time intervals without interrupting the actual CRM application.

Data Storage

Once the data has been ingested from various data sources, all the data is stored in a data lake. The data residing within the lake will still be in a raw format and includes both structured and unstructured data formats. At this point, the data won't bring much value to drive business insights.

Data Pipeline Orchestration & Monitoring

In a modern data warehouse scenario, it is very important that data sources and services efficiently transfer data from source to destination. Azure Data Factory is an orchestrator that allows services to perform the data migration or transfer. It is not the one performing the actual transfer, but rather instructs a service to perform it—for example, a Hadoop Cluster to perform a Hive query.

Azure Data Factory also allows you to create alerts and metrics to notify you when the service orchestration is working. You can create an alert via email, in case a data transfer was not successful from source to destination.

Data Sharing

In a modern data warehouse pattern, sharing data should be both seamless and secure. Often times this can be done via FTP (File Transport Protocol), emails, or APIs just to name a few. There is a big management overhead if you want to share data at scale. Azure Data Share allows you to securely manage and share your big data to other parties and organizations. The data provider will have full control of who can access the data sets and the permissions each can perform. This makes it easier for the dependent companies to derive insights and explore AI scenarios.

Data Preparation

Once data is ingested, the next step is data preparation. This is a phase where the data from different data sources is pre-processed for data analytics purposes. An example of this is querying data from an API and inserting them to a database table. Azure Data Factory allows you to orchestrate this data preparation. Azure Databricks can also help with data preparation, as it can run clusters concurrently to process massive amounts of data in just a matter of seconds or minutes.

Data Transform, Predict, & Enrich

Sometimes, the data preparation requires further changes beyond a simple "copy-and-paste" scenario. This is where Data Transformation comes in. There are instances wherein you want to apply custom logic in the raw data first—applying filters, for instance—before you decide to transfer it to a data warehouse. Azure Data Factory and Azure Databricks can also help in this scenario.

Furthermore, you can enrich the batch data at scale by invoking an Azure Machine Learning Service that makes real-time predictions about the data. This can be performed as an added feature in your data pipeline in Azure Data Factory. To learn more about Azure Machine Learning Service, see *Chapter 3, Processing and Visualizing Data*.

Data Serve

After preparing and training your data, you'll be ready to model and serve it to the consumers. Basically, in this phase, you are modeling the data to be easily understood by systems. This usually involves performing the complex queries you generated from the data preparation and training phase, and inserting these records into a database so that the data is structured in a defined table and schema.

All of your company's analytical data is stored in a data warehouse. You potentially have hundreds to thousands of concurrent users, reports, and dashboards running off a single data warehouse.

You usually perform Data Modeling and Service Integrations with a data warehouse platform such as Microsoft Azure Synapse Analytics. Complex and complete queries can take hours or days. But with the power of the cloud, you can scale your Azure Synapse Analytics to perform these queries faster, making days into hours and hours into minutes (more details on this in *Chapter 2, Building Your Modern Data Warehouse*).

Data Visualization

Data visualization is an efficient way of analyzing performance through graphs and charts. This is called business intelligence. Tools such as Power BI help analysts to get the most out of data. Data visualization provides a rich and meaningful representation of your data that adds business value for you and your customers. The team can see trends, outliers, and patterns which help in making data-driven decisions.

Various stakeholders within the organization can collaborate after analyzing the different performance parameters. Is your company selling products well? In what regions do you get most of your sales? With rich data backing up your assumptions, business stakeholders, such as CEOs can make reasonable data-driven decisions to minimize risks. What product lines should you expand? Where should you expand further? These are some of the common questions that you can answer once you have richer data analytics.

Analysts can use desktop or web application tools to create meaningful representations of their data. Below is a sample of a desktop view of Power BI where a user can perform analysis of their company's data and visualize it in graphs:

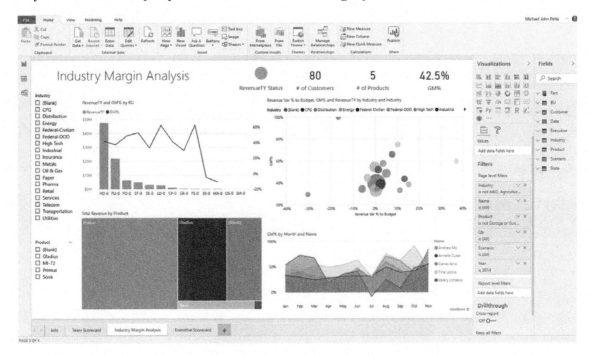

Figure 1.6: Power BI dashboard on desktop

Once the reports are generated, they can be exported to a workspace where people can work together to improve the reports. Below is a sample view of the same report in a mobile application. Users can add comments and annotations to the report, allowing a faster feedback loop for analysts:

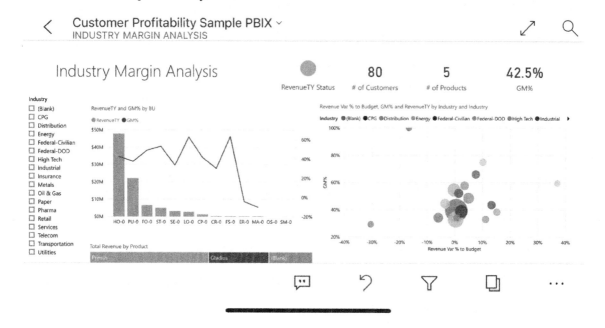

Figure 1.7: Power BI dashboard for mobile

Power BI allows you to create rich personalized dashboards that best suit your requirements and brand. Compared to having presentations with a snapshot of a graph from last week or last month, this mechanism allows you to refresh the same report over and over again.

Smarter Applications

Machine learning has helped companies build applications and products such as chatbots that perform specific tasks for end users without the need for human intervention. Some common examples are voice assistants, such as Cortana, which actively learn to help us become more productive with our day-to-day tasks.

Other examples are online games in which you can easily track your performance against everyone in the world. You can better understand how you rank against other players, what areas you excel in, what needs improvement, and how you can improve.

The number of tasks you can do with rich data are virtually limitless, but in order to perform them, you need to have the right approach and infrastructure to handle a high level of scaling.

Summary

This chapter established the importance of data analytics. It also highlighted several reasons why Microsoft Azure is an ideal platform of choice for achieving business intelligence capabilities on the cloud. It also touched on some fundamental concepts around big data, machine learning, and DataOps. You also learned some of the business drivers for adopting data analytics on the cloud. Lastly, you gained a high-level view of what it takes to have a modern data warehouse.

In the next chapter, you will see how to start building modern data warehouse with Azure Data Factory, Azure Databricks, Azure Data Lake, Azure Synapse Analytics, and related technologies.

Building Your Modern Data Warehouse

In recent years, big data has been gaining significant traction around the world. With such a massive volume of data, there is a need to have specialized platforms, tools, and storage in order to process and analyze it.

In *Chapter 1, Introducing Analytics on Azure*, you were introduced to Azure and learned about the types of platforms, tools, and resources that Azure provides to facilitate the creation of data warehouse solutions.

This chapter will delve further into each of the four key technologies which follow:

- Azure Synapse Analytics (formerly known as Azure SQL Data Warehouse)

- Azure Data Factory

- Azure Data Lake Storage Gen2

- Azure Databricks

By the end of this chapter, you will gain a better understanding of how you can use these technologies to build your own modern data warehouse solution. So, strap on your seat belt as we begin our tour.

What is a Modern Data Warehouse?

A modern data warehouse allows you to ingest data from various data sources at any scale, whether on-premises or in the cloud, to produce valuable insights for your business. The benefit of a modern data warehouse is that the data source can be structured, semi-structured, or unstructured data. Examples of each are provided in the following figure:

Type of Data Source	Examples
Structured Data	Purchase transactions in a database
Semi-structured Data	Log files with events and trace messages from the application server
Unstructured Data	Natural language posts from social media feeds (e.g. Twitter, Facebook, etc.)

Figure 2.1: Examples of different data source types

Here is a typical architectural and data flow diagram of a modern data warehouse:

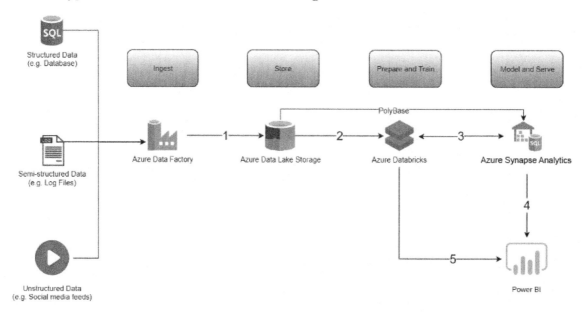

Figure 2.2: Modern data warehouse architecture

The architectural and data flow is as follows:

1. The modern data warehouse life cycle begins with the ingestion phase. You can amalgamate data from various sources, whether they are structured, semi-structured, or unstructured, using **Azure Data Factory** and store the data in **Azure Data Lake Storage Gen2**.

2. For data preparation, you can cleanse and transform the data stored in **Azure Data Lake Storage Gen2** by doing scalable analytics using **Azure Databricks**.

3. After completely cleaning and transforming the data, it can now be appended to the existing data in the Azure warehouse database. You can query or move this data using connectors between the **Azure Synapse Analytics** and the **Azure Databricks**.

4. The data prepared as mentioned in *point* 3 can be consumed in the form of reports or some kind of dashboards for data analytics.

5. To complete the modern data warehouse workflow, you can run ad hoc queries on the data directly within **Azure Databricks** and visualize the results in **Power BI**. (This will be covered in Chapter 3, Processing and Visualizing Data.)

In this chapter, you will specifically focus on *steps* 1, 2, and 3. *Steps* 4 and 5 will be covered in the next chapter.

The following sections will introduce you to each of these Azure services outlined above, including their respective features and benefits.

Azure Synapse Analytics

Azure Synapse Analytics (formerly known as Azure SQL Data Warehouse) is a limitless analytics service which amalgamates warehouse and big data at enterprise level. It has the capacity to perform massive data processing simultaneously. In this section, you will have a look at the features that Azure Synapse Analytics offers and its benefits. Later in this chapter, you will learn how to provision your own Azure Synapse Analytics in the Quick Start Guide.

Features

Azure Synapse Analytics provides the following features:

- Ability to run up to 128 queries concurrently using Massively Parallel Processing (MPP)

- Separated compute and storage

- The most cost-effective cloud data warehouse

- Ability to stop databases temporarily, and resume them again within a few seconds

- Ability to build your own jobs and hub smoothly with any connectors for data integration and visualization services

- Compatibility with data laws in more than 30 countries across the world

- Inbuilt data caching, which cultivates faster data querying and performance

Benefits

Azure Synapse Analytics provides you with the following benefits:

- Ease of scalability in accordance with your workload requirements

- Cost-efficiency due to Azure's 'pay as you go' concept

- Guarantee of 99.9% availability

Azure Data Factory

Azure Data Factory (ADF) is a fully managed, highly scalable, highly available, and easy-to-use tool for creating integration solutions and implementing Extract-Transform-Load (ETL) phases.

Once the data is ingested, Azure Data Factory allows you to push the data, using its native data connector, to Azure Data Lake Storage Gen2. You can easily create new pipelines in Azure Data Factory using a drag-and-drop approach without writing any code. For advanced implementation, you can write custom code in your preferred languages to customize Azure Data Factory to further meet your specific needs.

Azure Data Factory simplifies data integration for users of all skill levels.

Features

Azure Data Factory provides the following features:

- Ability to connect to various data sources whether they are on-premises or in the cloud
- Ability to move data from both on-premises and cloud data stores to a centralized data store on Azure using the Copy Activity in the data pipeline
- Code-free ingestion
- Code-free data transformation
- Ability to process and transform the data from a centralized data store on Azure
- A controlled schedule to create one trusted data source to be consumed by production environments
- Ability to transform and cleanse data and load it into Azure Synapse Analytics to be consumed by business intelligence tools and analytics engines
- Quality-assurance through continuous pipeline-monitoring
- Inbuilt monitoring features like Azure Monitor or Azure PowerShell for managing resources

Benefits

Azure Data Factory provides you with the following benefits:

- Orchestration of other Azure services. For example, Azure Data Factory can call stored procedure in Azure Synapse Analytics or run Azure Databricks notebooks.

- Fully managed and server-less

- Easy-to-use tool for creating integration solutions

- Highly scalable. The following table illustrates the copy duration achieved by Azure Data Factory based on data size and bandwidth:

Data size / Bandwidth	50 Mbps	100 Mbps	500 Mbps	1 Gbps	5 Gbps	10 Gbps	50 Gbps
1 GB	2.7 min	1.4 min	0.3 min	0.1 min	0.03 min	0.01 min	0.0 min
10 GB	27.3 min	13.7 min	2.7 min	1.3 min	0.3 min	0.1 min	0.03 min
100 GB	4.6 hrs	2.3 hrs	0.5 hrs	0.2 hrs	0.05 hrs	0.02 hrs	0.0 hrs
1 TB	46.6 hrs	23.3 hrs	4.7 hrs	2.3 hrs	0.5 hrs	0.2 hrs	0.05 hrs
10 TB	19.4 days	9.7 days	1.9 days	0.9 days	0.2 days	0.1 days	0.02 days
100 TB	194.2 days	97.1 days	19.4 days	9.7 days	1.9 days	1 days	0.2 days
1 PB	64.7 mo	32.4 mo	6.5 mo	3.2 mo	0.6 mo	0.3 mo	0.06 mo
10 PB	647.3 mo	323.6 mo	64.7 mo	31.6 mo	6.5 mo	3.2 mo	0.6 mo

Figure 2.3: ADF copy duration based on data size and bandwidth

Azure Data Lake Storage Gen2

Azure Data Lake Storage Gen2 offers low-cost scalable data storage solutions built from Azure Blob Storage technology. Specifically designed for big data analytics, Azure Data Lake Storage Gen2 allows users to store structured, semi-structured, and unstructured data from various sources. These sources include relational databases, Customer Relationship Management (CRM) systems, mobile applications, desktop applications, IoT devices, and more.

Structured data stored in Azure Data Lake Storage Gen2 can be loaded into Azure Synapse Analytics using Azure Data Factory, Azure Databricks, PolyBase or the COPY command.

Features

Azure Data Lake Storage Gen2 provides the following features:

- Data access and management through Hadoop Distributed File System (HDFS)

- Azure Blob Filesystem (ABFS) driver, which allows data access to Azure Data Lake Storage Gen2 from all Apache Hadoop environments, such as Azure Synapse Analytics, Azure Databricks and Azure HDInsight, Azure Databricks

- Support for ACL and POSIX permissions, in addition to extra Azure Data Lake Storage Gen2 permissions

- Configurable settings through Azure Storage Explorer, Apache Spark and Apache Hive

- Secure (and cost-effective) scalability of storage at file level

- High availability/disaster recovery (HA/DR) capabilities

Benefits

Azure Data Lake Storage Gen2 offers the following benefits:

- Support for applications that implement the open Apache Hadoop Distributed File System (HDFS) standard

- Low-cost storage capacity and transactions

Azure Databricks

Azure Databricks is an analytics platform based on Apache Spark which allows you to implement artificial intelligence solutions and collaborate insights using an interactive workspace. It supports languages such as Python, Java, R, Scala, and SQL, along with a variety of data science tools—for example, TensorFlow, scikit-learn, and PyTorch.

Features

Azure Databricks provides the following features:

- Interactive and collaborative workspace.

- Full Apache Spark cluster capabilities with components such as Spark SQL and DataFrames, Mlib, GraphX and Spark Core API.

Benefits

Azure Databricks offers the following benefits:

- Easy set-up of fully-managed Apache Spark clusters on Azure.

- Zero-management cloud platform.

- Interactive and collaborative workspace for exploration and visualization.

- Fast cluster creation.

- Dynamic auto-scaling of clusters, including server-less clusters.

- Operation of clusters using code and the APIs.

- Capacity to integrate data securely based on Apache Spark.

- Instant access to the most up-to-date Apache Spark features with each release.

- Native integration with Azure Synapse Analytics, Azure Data Lake Storage, Azure Cosmos DB, Azure Blob Storage, and Power BI.

Quick Start Guide

In this quick start guide, you will provision your first Azure Synapse Analytics (formerly SQL DW). You will populate your data warehouse with a sample database called AdventureWorksDW. Afterwards, you will connect your database and run SQL queries to get results from your data.

And finally, you will pause your Azure SQL Data Warehouse (also known as Azure Synapse Analytics) to stop the compute billing when you no longer need to use the data warehouse (you will only be charged for storage, in this case).

> **Note**
>
> At the time of publishing, Microsoft is evolving **Azure SQL Data Warehouse** to **Azure Synapse Analytics**. As such, certain steps in this guide will refer to the new name, **Azure Synapse Analytics,** while other steps will show the original name, **Azure SQL Data Warehouse**. Please visit https://packt.live/2puhcEA for the latest updates.

Provision Your First Azure Synapse Analytics (formerly SQL DW)

Perform the following steps to provision your data warehouse:

1. In a web browser, sign into the Azure Portal (http://portal.azure.com/).

2. Click **Create a resource** in the upper left-hand corner of the Azure Portal:

Figure 2.4: Creating a resource on Azure Portal

3. Select **Databases** under the **Azure Marketplace** section in the **New** page, and choose **Azure Synapse Analytics (formerly SQL DW)** from the **Featured** section:

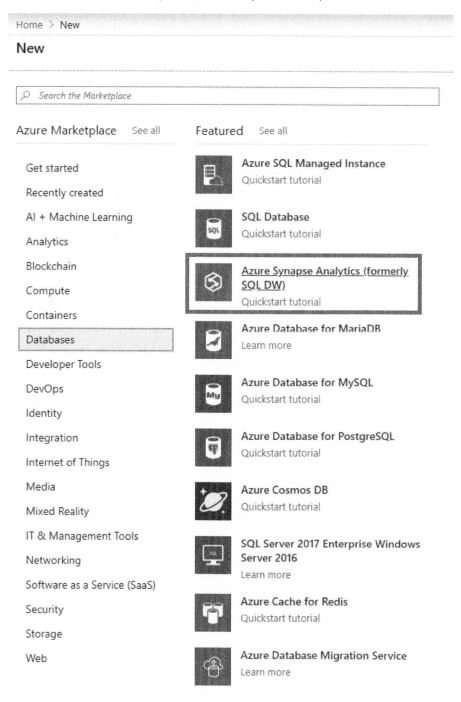

Figure 2.5: Creating a new Azure Synapse Analytics (formerly SQL DW)

4. Fill out all project details in the **SQL Data Warehouse** form, as shown in the following figure:

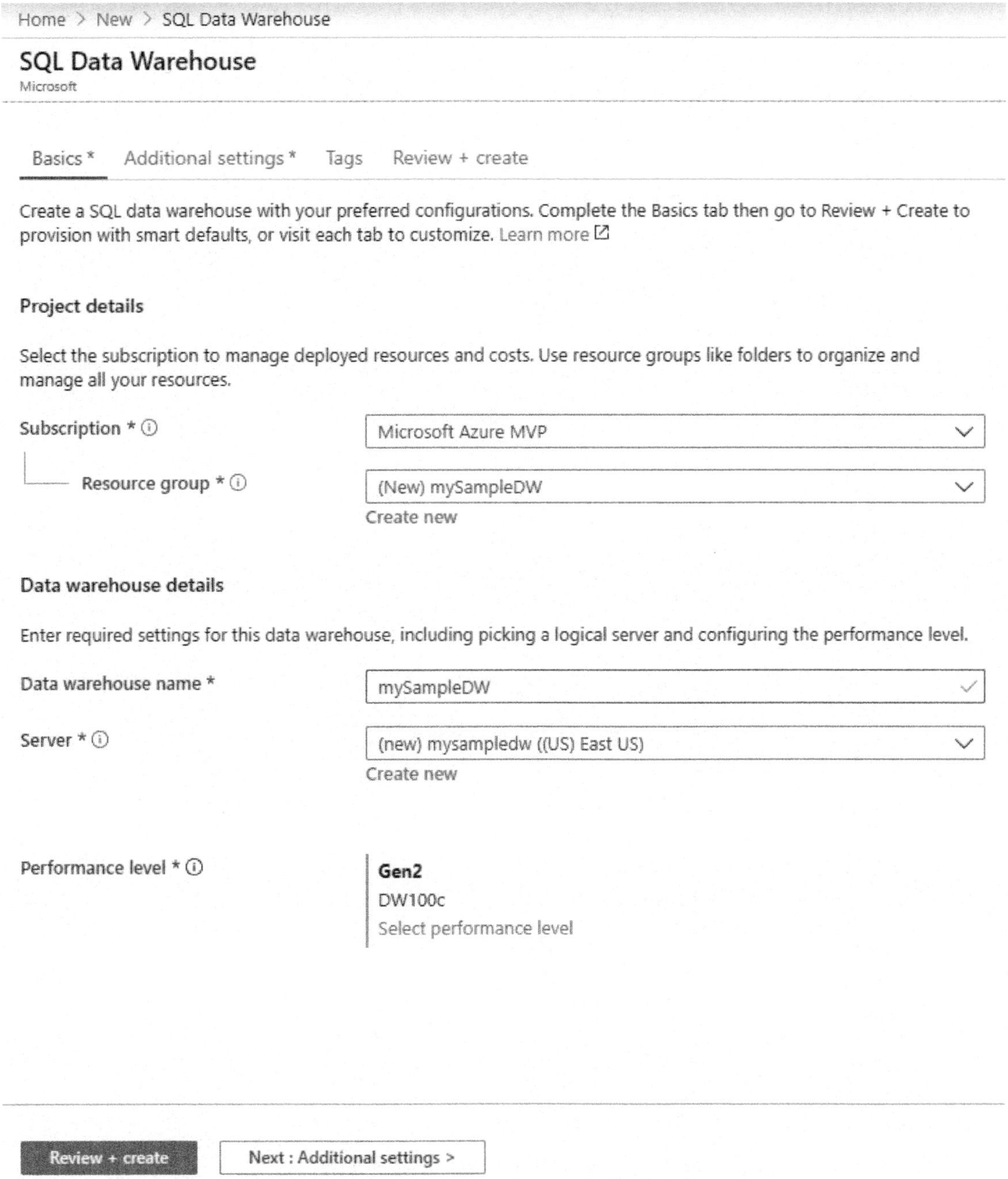

Home > New > SQL Data Warehouse

SQL Data Warehouse
Microsoft

Basics *   Additional settings *   Tags   Review + create

Create a SQL data warehouse with your preferred configurations. Complete the Basics tab then go to Review + Create to provision with smart defaults, or visit each tab to customize. Learn more

Project details

Select the subscription to manage deployed resources and costs. Use resource groups like folders to organize and manage all your resources.

Subscription * ⓘ | Microsoft Azure MVP   ⌄ |

        Resource group * ⓘ | (New) mySampleDW   ⌄ |
                                     Create new

Data warehouse details

Enter required settings for this data warehouse, including picking a logical server and configuring the performance level.

Data warehouse name * | mySampleDW   ✓ |

Server * ⓘ | (new) mysampledw ((US) East US)   ⌄ |
                                     Create new

Performance level * ⓘ   **Gen2**
                                    DW100c
                                    Select performance level

[Review + create]   [Next : Additional settings >]

Figure 2.6: Adding project details to the data warehouse

The suggested value and explanation of each is shown in the following table:

Setting	Suggested Value	Description
Subscription	Your Azure subscription	Pick your Azure subscription
Resource Group	mySampleDW	Create a new Resource Group called mySampleRG.
Data warehouse name	mySampleDW	Use any valid database name.
Select source	Sample	Specify to load a sample database.
Select sample	AdventureWorksDW	Specify to load the AdventureWorksDW sample database
Performance Level	Gen2, DW100c	Specify the data warehouse performance level.
Location	East US	Specify the location of your data warehouse and associated resources.

Figure 2.7: Project setting details

5. Under **Data warehouse details**, **Server**, click **Create new**. This will open the following blade. Provide server details such as **Server name**, **Server admin login**, **Password**, and **Location** accordingly:

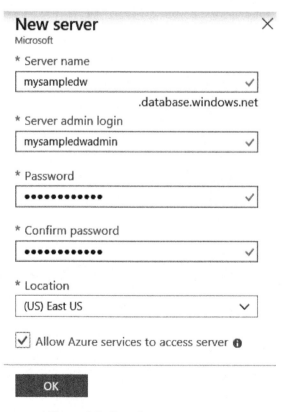

Figure 2.8: Creating a new server

6. Select **Performance level** and select **Gen2**. In this example, you will scale your system to **DW100c**. Click **Apply** to commit the selection.

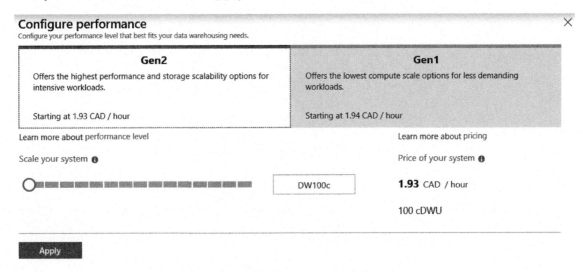

Figure 2.9: Selecting performance levels

7. Click **Next: Additional settings**

Home > New > SQL Data Warehouse

SQL Data Warehouse
Microsoft

Project details

Select the subscription to manage deployed resources and costs. Use resource groups like folders to organize and manage all your resources.

* Subscription ❶	Microsoft Azure MVP ⌄
└─ * Resource group ❶	(New) mySampleDW ⌄
	Create new

Data warehouse details

Enter required settings for this data warehouse, including picking a logical server and configuring the performance level.

* Data warehouse name	mySampleDW ✓
* Server ❶	(new) mysampledw ((US) East US) ⌄
	Create new
* Performance level ❶	**Gen2**
	DW100c
	Select performance level

Review + create	Next : Additional settings >

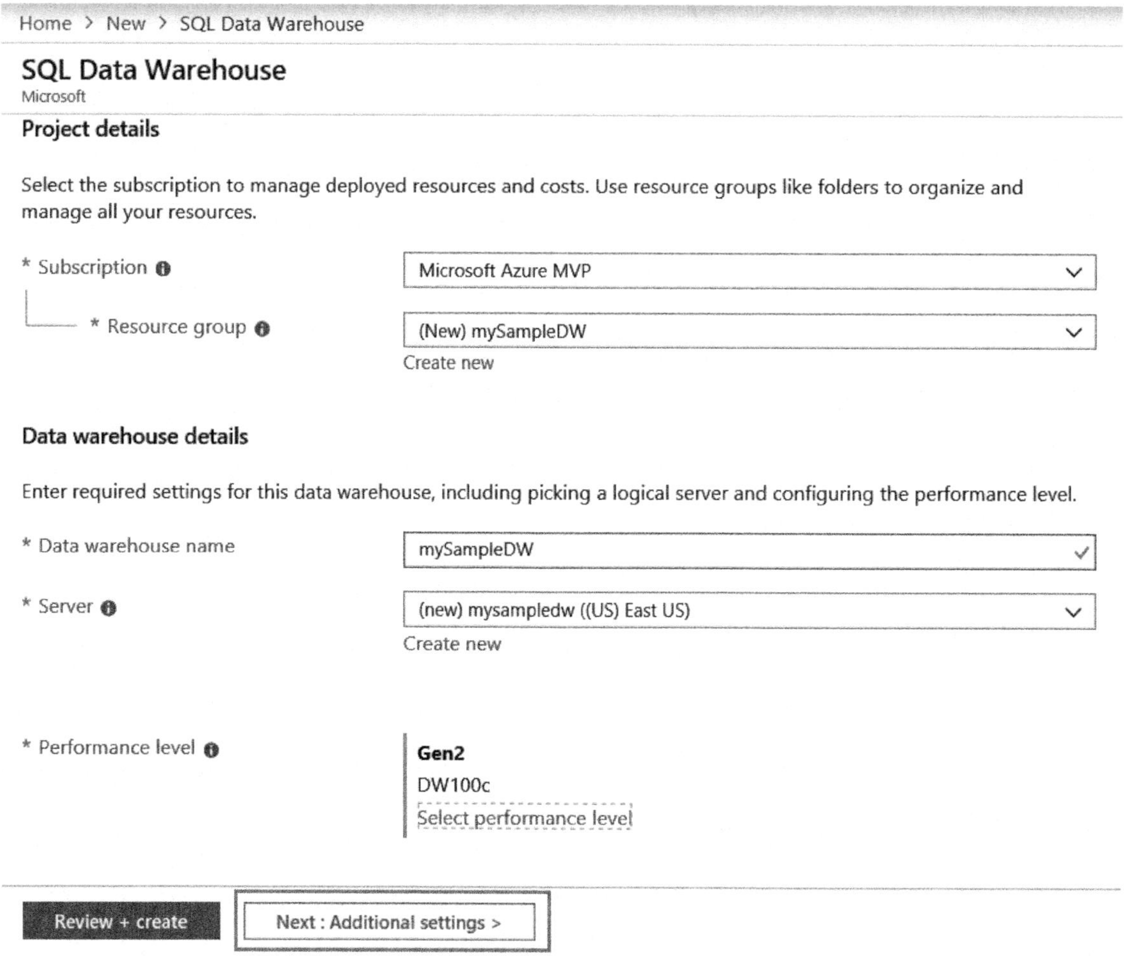

Figure 2.10: Configuring additional settings

8. For your Quick Start Tour, set **Use existing data** to **Sample**. This will load the **AdventureWorksDW** sample database into your newly created data warehouse. Click **Review + create** to continue.

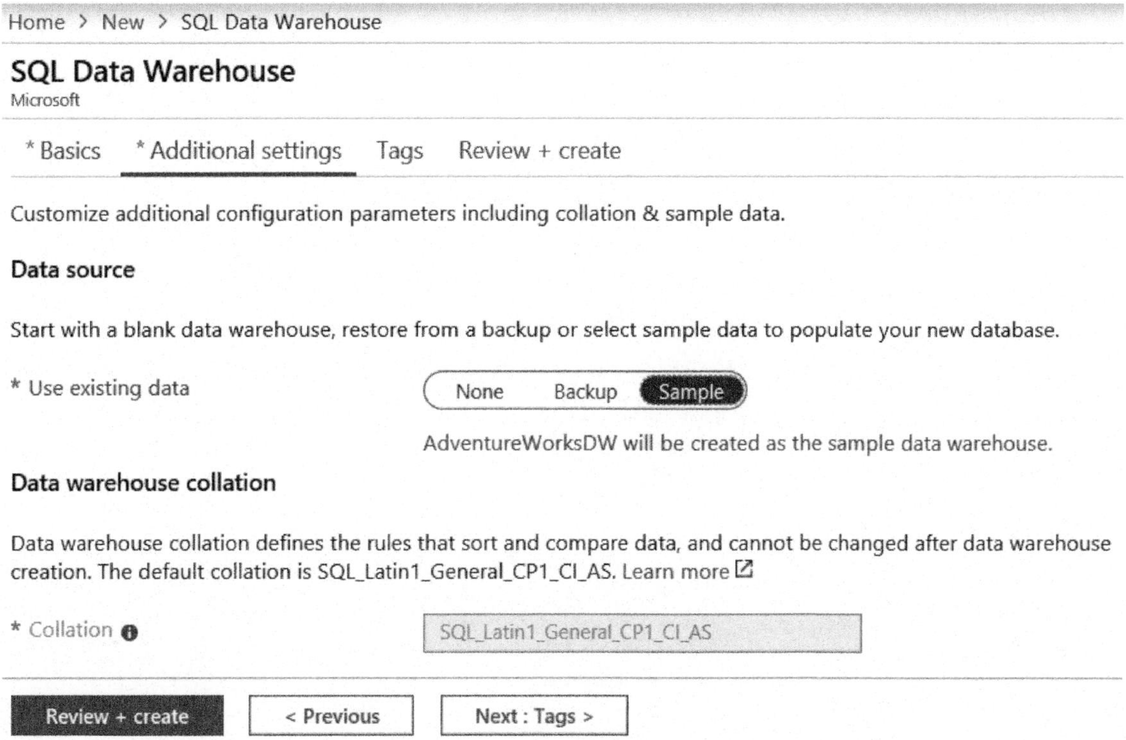

Home > New > SQL Data Warehouse

SQL Data Warehouse
Microsoft

* Basics   * Additional settings   Tags   Review + create

Customize additional configuration parameters including collation & sample data.

Data source

Start with a blank data warehouse, restore from a backup or select sample data to populate your new database.

* Use existing data   None   Backup   Sample

AdventureWorksDW will be created as the sample data warehouse.

Data warehouse collation

Data warehouse collation defines the rules that sort and compare data, and cannot be changed after data warehouse creation. The default collation is SQL_Latin1_General_CP1_CI_AS. Learn more ⎘

* Collation ⓘ   SQL_Latin1_General_CP1_CI_AS

Review + create   < Previous   Next : Tags >

Figure 2.11: Using sample dataset for Quick Start Guide

9. Do a final review and then click **Create** to start provisioning your SQL Data Warehouse:

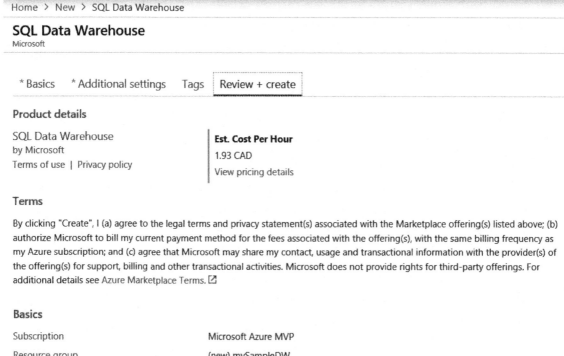

Figure 2.12: Creating your SQL data warehouse

10. While your new SQL Data Warehouse is being provisioned, you can monitor its deployment progress:

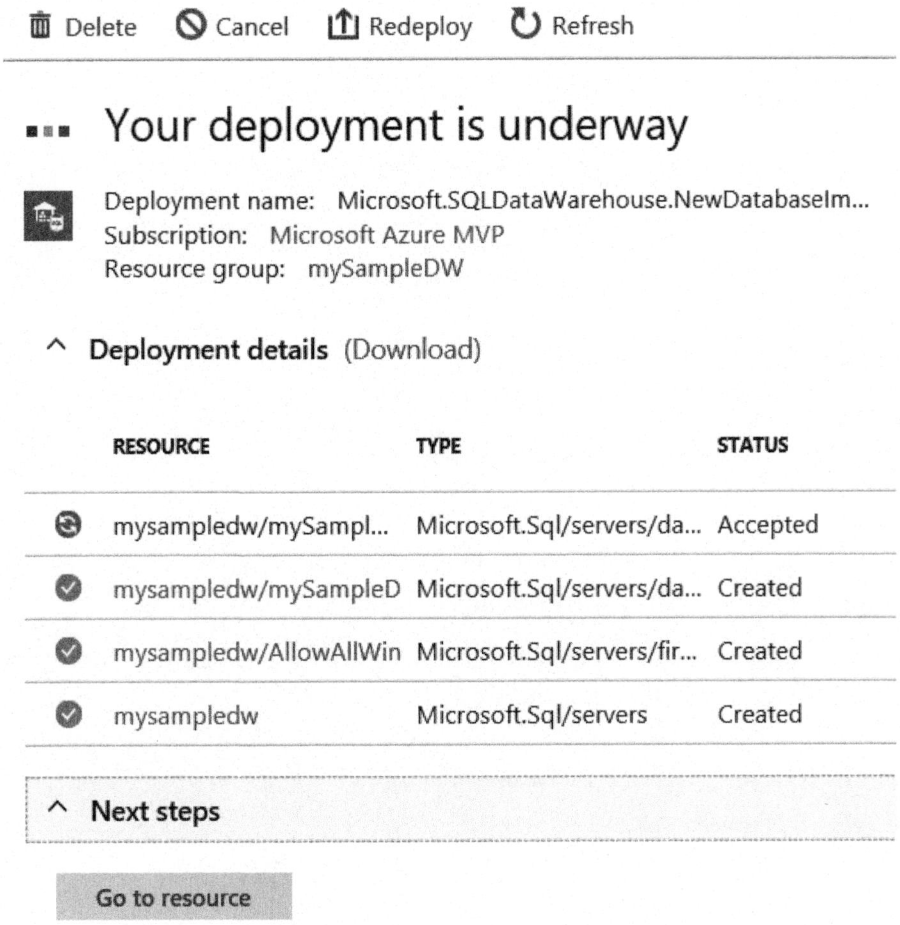

🗑 Delete   ⊘ Cancel   ⬆ Redeploy   ↻ Refresh

▪▪▪ Your deployment is underway

Deployment name: Microsoft.SQLDataWarehouse.NewDatabaseIm...
Subscription: Microsoft Azure MVP
Resource group: mySampleDW

∧ **Deployment details** (Download)

	RESOURCE	TYPE	STATUS
🔄	mysampledw/mySampl...	Microsoft.Sql/servers/da...	Accepted
✅	mysampledw/mySampleD	Microsoft.Sql/servers/da...	Created
✅	mysampledw/AllowAllWin	Microsoft.Sql/servers/fir...	Created
✅	mysampledw	Microsoft.Sql/servers	Created

∧   Next steps

Go to resource

Figure 2.13: Monitoring data warehouse deployment

11. Once deployment is complete, you will see the following screen:

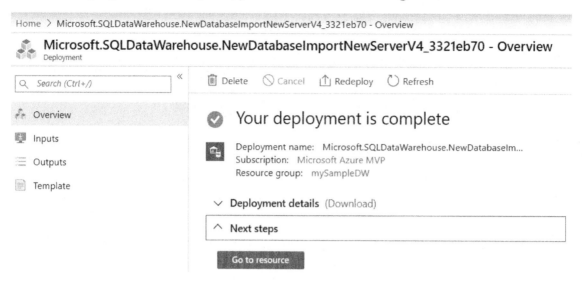

Figure 2.14: Data warehouse deployment completed

You have successfully provisioned your first Azure Synapse Analytics (formerly known as Azure SQL Data Warehouse).

If you go to your resource group named mySampleDW, you will see the following resources which have been successfully provisioned:

Figure 2.15: List of provisioned resources

Querying the Data

You can use the **Query editor (preview)** built into the Azure Portal to query the data. This is extremely convenient. Perform the following steps to query the data:

1. Click **Query editor (preview)** from `mySampleDW` database. You will then see the following screen. Simply provide the login and password information which you entered earlier when you provisioned your Azure Synapse Analytics (formerly known as Azure SQL Data Warehouse):

Welcome to SQL Database Query Editor

SQL server authentication

* Login

mysampledwadmin

* Password

••••••••••• ✓

◯ Logging in as mysampledwadmin...

OK

Figure 2.16: SQL Database Query Editor

> **Note**
>
> If you receive an error such as "Cannot open server 'mysampledw' requested by the login. Client with IP address 'xx.xx.xx.xx' is not allowed to access the server", simply follow the instructions in the *Whitelisting Your Client IP Address to Access Your Azure Synapse Analytics (formerly SQL DW)* section to whitelist your client IP address. After your client IP address has been whitelisted, you can retry step 1.

2. Once you logged into your data warehouse database, you can execute SQL queries to retrieve the information that you need. Enter the following query in the Query pane, then click **Run**:

```
select firstname, lastname, phone
from dimCustomer
order by lastname
```

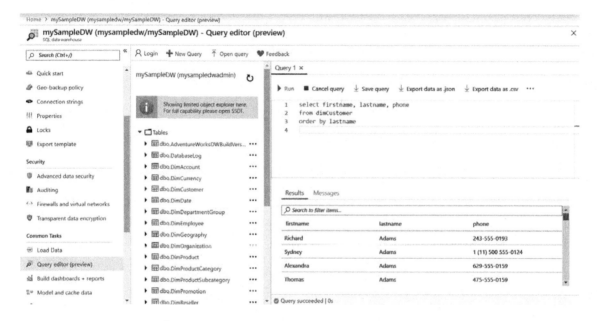

Figure 2.17: Executing queries in the query editor

3. Try another query, and click **Run**:

```
select firstname, lastname, phone
from dimCustomer
where lastname = 'Lee'
order by firstname
```

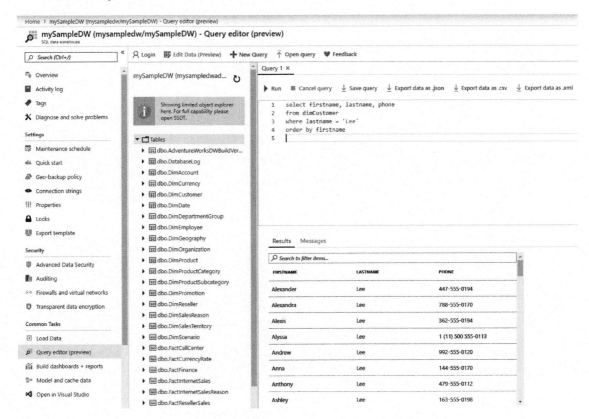

Figure 2.18: Executing queries in the query editor

Feel free to try other queries on your own.

Whitelisting Your Client IP Address to Access Your Azure Synapse Analytics (formerly SQL DW)

If you wish to access your Azure Synapse Analytics (formerly SQL DW) from your local SQL Server Management Studio (SMSS) or from the Query editor (preview), you will need to add a server-side firewall rule that enables connectivity for your client IP address by following these steps:

1. Under **Security**, go to **Firewalls and virtual networks**. Click **Add client IP** to whitelist your current IP address. Then, click **Save**:

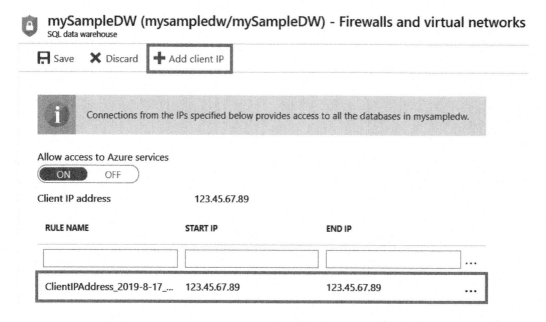

Figure 2.19: Adding Client IP address

2. Next, go to your SQL Data Warehouse, **Overview**, and attain your **Server name**.

Figure 2.20: Copying the server name

3. With your client IP address whitelisted, you can now connect to your Azure Synapse Analytics (formerly SQL DW) from your local SSMS or from the Query editor (preview) by simply connecting with your Server name, username and password.

Pause your Azure Synapse Analytics when not in use

When you are not using your Azure Synapse Analytics (formerly SQL Data Warehouse), it is a good idea to pause it to avoid being billed for additional compute charges. The advantage of pausing your data warehouse rather than deleting it is that when you are ready to continue working, you can simply resume your data warehouse without having to re-provision it all over again.

> **Note**
>
> When your Azure SQL Data Warehouse is paused, even though you do not have to pay for any compute charges, you will still be responsible for any storage charges.

Figure 2.21: Pausing your data warehouse

Once your Azure SQL Data Warehouse is paused, its status will show paused:

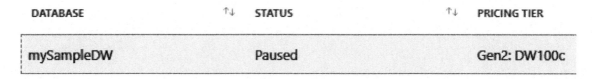

Figure 2.22: SQL Data Warehouse status

When you are ready to work on your Azure SQL Data Warehouse again, simply click **Resume**:

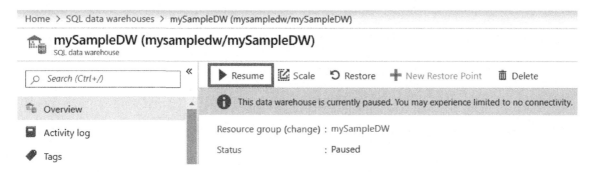

Figure 2.23: Resuming your data warehouse

Provisioning your Azure Data Factory

Now that you have provisioned your first Azure Synapse Analytics (formerly known as Azure Data Warehouse), you can provision your Azure Data Factory, as outlined in the following steps:

1. Click **Create a resource** in the upper left-hand corner of the Azure Portal:

Figure 2.24: Creating your resource

2. Select **Analytics** under the Azure Marketplace section in **New** page, and choose **Data Factory** from the **Featured** section

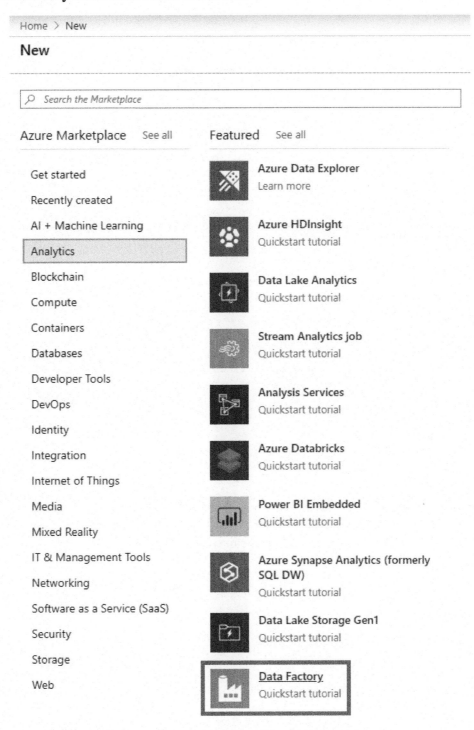

Figure 2.25: Selecting Azure Data Factory

3. Fill out the **New data factory** form as shown in the following figure:

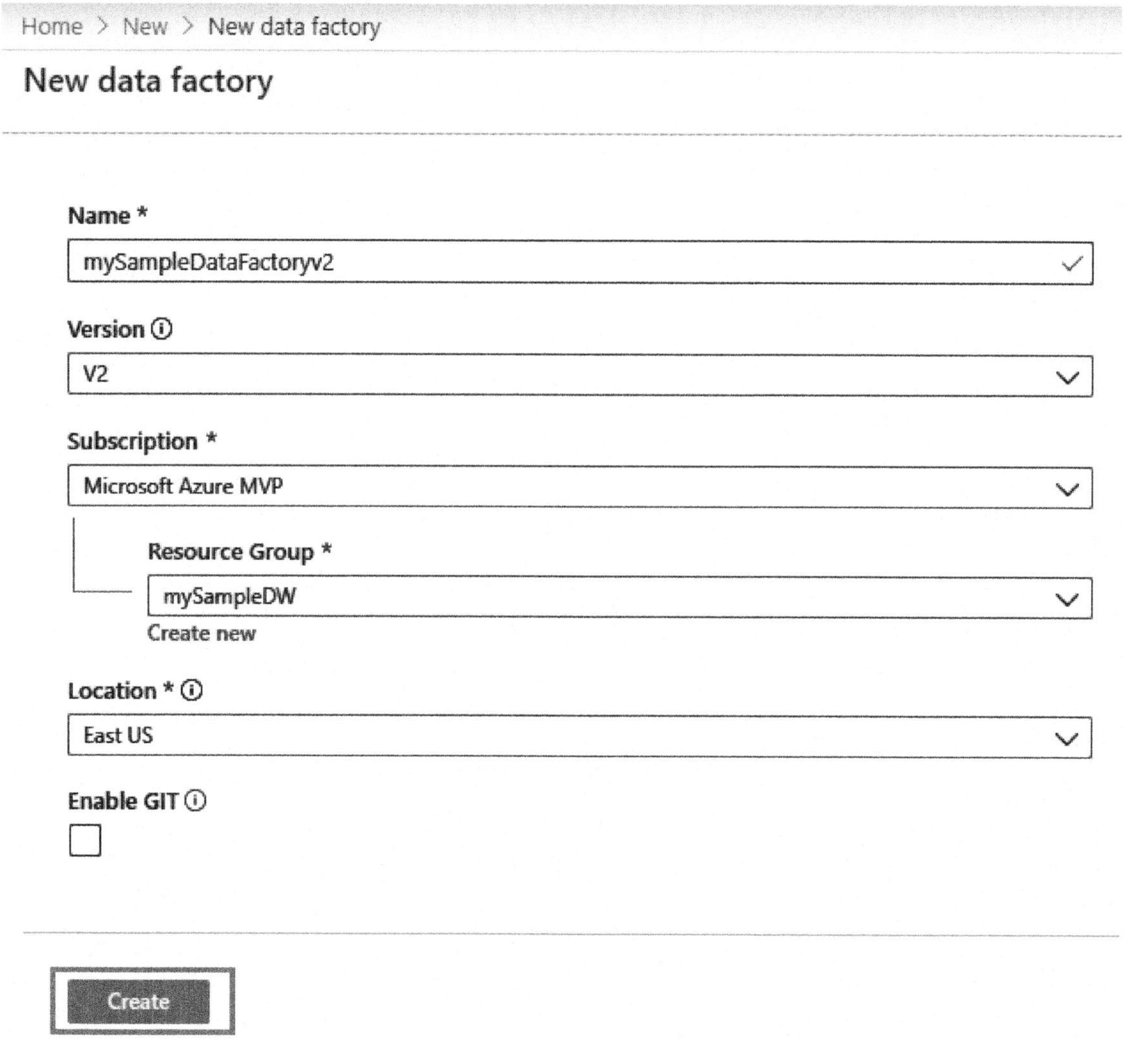

Figure 2.26: Adding details to create the data factory

The suggested values and their explanation are provided below:

Setting	Suggested Value	Description
Name	mySampleDataFactoryv2	Specify a globally unique name for your Azure Data Factory. If the name is taken, try a different name.
Subscription	Your Azure subscription	Pick your Azure subscription
Resource Group	mySampleDW	Select the Resource Group which we created when we provisioned our Azure SQL Data Warehouse
Version	V2	Pick Data Factory V2.
Location	East US	Select the location of the Data Factory.

Figure 2.27: Suggested values for data factory creation

4. Click **Create** to start provisioning your Azure Data Factory.

Now that you have successfully provisioned your Azure Data Factory, the next step is to provision your Azure Data Lake Storage Gen2. You will later integrate the two technologies in another exercise.

Provision Your Azure Data Lake Storage Gen2

Next, follow these steps to provision your Azure Data Lake Storage Gen2:

1. Click **Create a resource** in the upper left-hand corner of the Azure Portal:

Figure 2.28: Creating a resource in the Azure portal

2. Select **Storage** under the Azure Marketplace section in the **New** page, and choose **Storage account** from the **Featured** section:

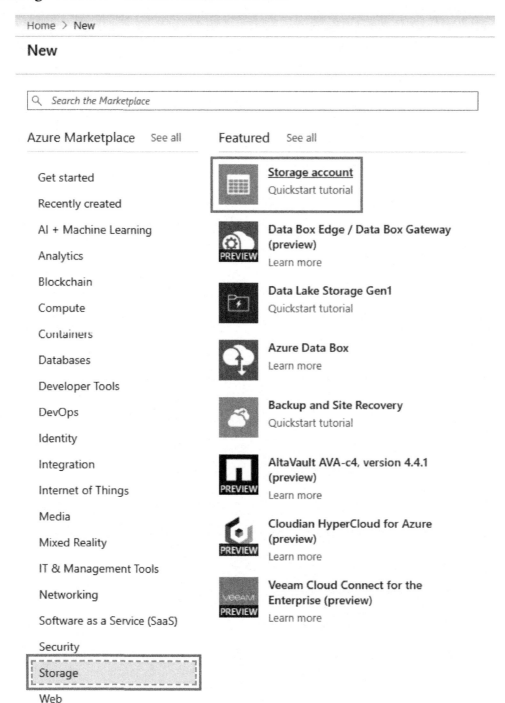

Figure 2.29: Creating a storage account

3. In the **Create storage account** form, populate with the information below. You will need to select your own subscription and provide a unique storage account name. For resource group, select the resource group previously created when you provisioned the Azure Synapse Analytics (formerly known as Azure SQL Data Warehouse).

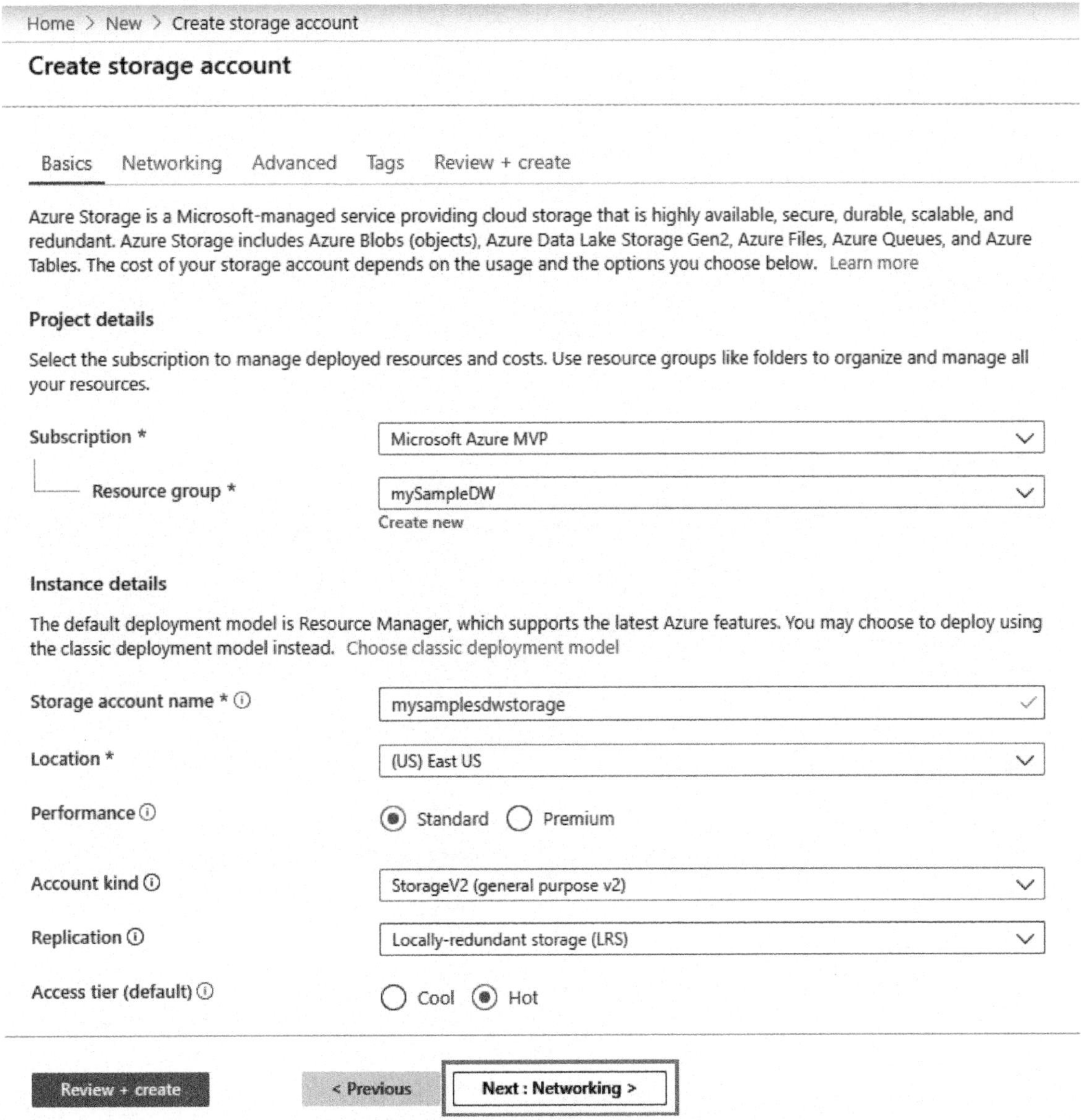

Home > New > Create storage account

Create storage account

Basics   Networking   Advanced   Tags   Review + create

Azure Storage is a Microsoft-managed service providing cloud storage that is highly available, secure, durable, scalable, and redundant. Azure Storage includes Azure Blobs (objects), Azure Data Lake Storage Gen2, Azure Files, Azure Queues, and Azure Tables. The cost of your storage account depends on the usage and the options you choose below. Learn more

Project details

Select the subscription to manage deployed resources and costs. Use resource groups like folders to organize and manage all your resources.

Subscription *	Microsoft Azure MVP
Resource group *	mySampleDW

Create new

Instance details

The default deployment model is Resource Manager, which supports the latest Azure features. You may choose to deploy using the classic deployment model instead. Choose classic deployment model

Storage account name * ⓘ	mysamplesdwstorage
Location *	(US) East US
Performance ⓘ	⦿ Standard ◯ Premium
Account kind ⓘ	StorageV2 (general purpose v2)
Replication ⓘ	Locally-redundant storage (LRS)
Access tier (default) ⓘ	◯ Cool ⦿ Hot

Review + create   < Previous   Next : Networking >

Figure 2.30: Storage account details

4. Set networking connectivity method to **Public endpoint (all networks)** and click the **Next: Advanced >** button.

5. In the **Data Lake Storage Gen2** section, set **Hierarchical namespace** to **Enabled**.
    Then click **Review + create**:

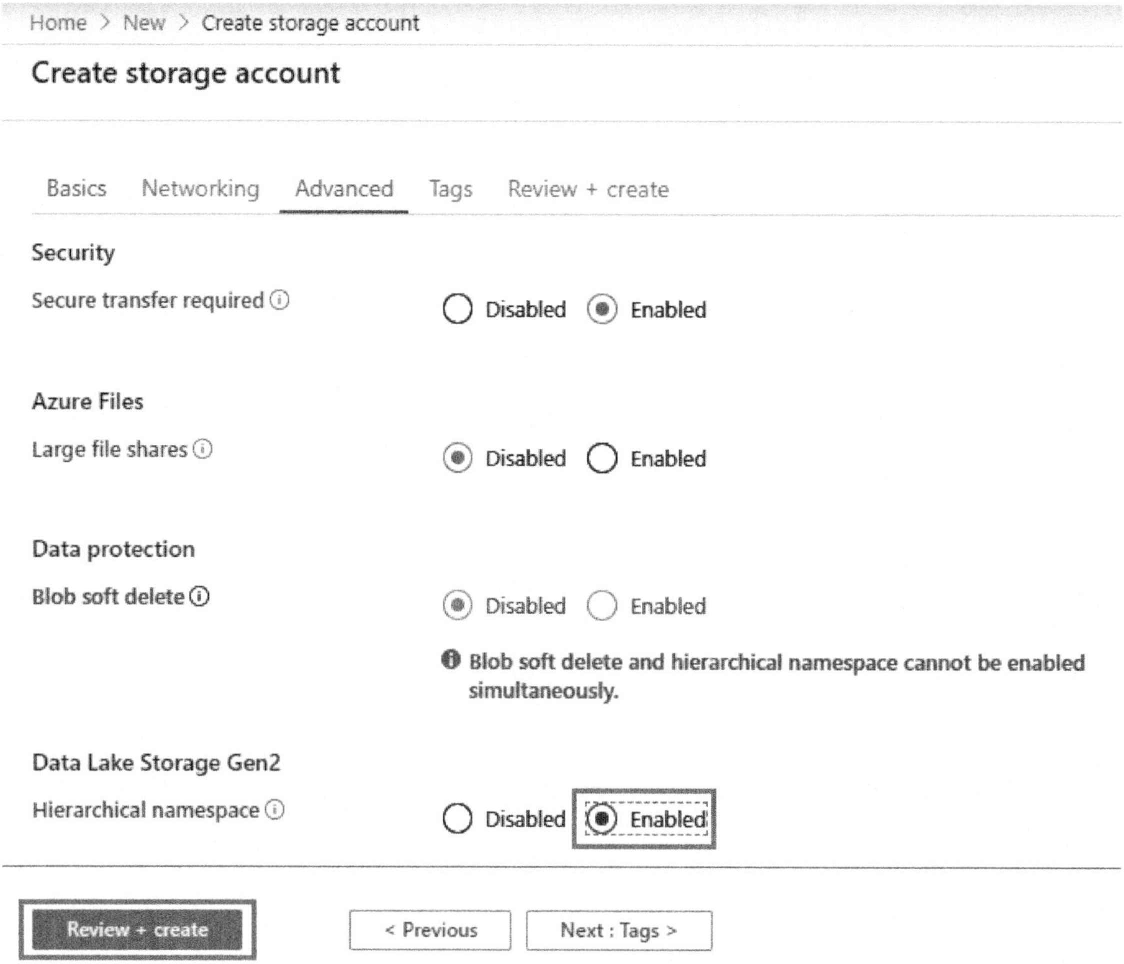

Figure 2.31: Enabling Data Lake Storage hierarchical namespace

6. Do a final review, then click **Create** to start provisioning your Azure Data Lake
    Storage Gen2 account.

As you can see from the step-by-step instructions above, creating an Azure Data Lake
Storage Gen2 is as straight-forward as creating an Azure Storage account.

Integrating Azure Data Factory with Azure Data Lake Storage Gen2

With the Azure Data Factory and the Azure Data Lake Storage Gen2 provisioned in the previous exercises, you are now ready to integrate the two technologies.

You will first ingest a **JSON** file using the Azure Data Factory, and extract the data and transform it into **CSV** file format. Then, load the resulting CSV formatted file into Azure Data Lake Storage Gen2.

1. Go to your Azure Data Factory and launch the Data Integration Application by clicking **Author & Monitor**:

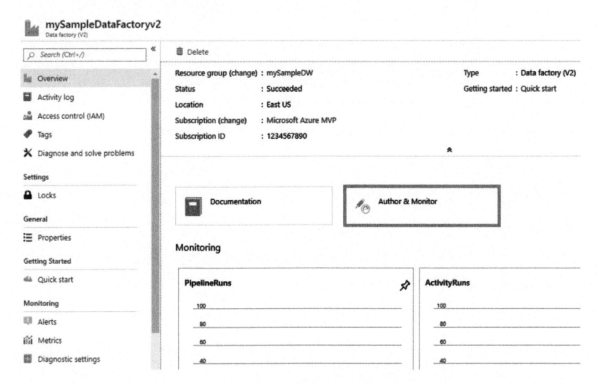

Figure 2.32: Launching the Data Integration Application

2. The Data Integration Application will launch in a separate browser tab. Click **Copy Data**:

Figure 2.33: Initiating the copy data task

3. Give your copy pipeline a **Task name** (and a **Task description**, if you wish), then click **Next**:

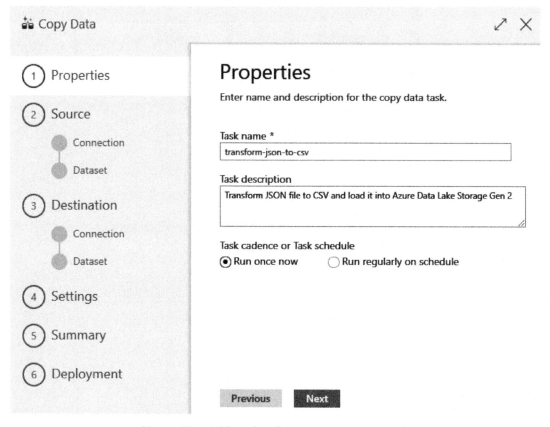

Figure 2.34: Adding details to the copy data task

The Azure Data Factory is comprised of dataset which is basically structured data in data store. A pipeline includes activities which are connected logically for accomplishing a task. A linked service allows you to connect Azure Data Factory to various data sources. In the next step, you will create a new linked Service for the new data source.

4. Click **Create new connection**:

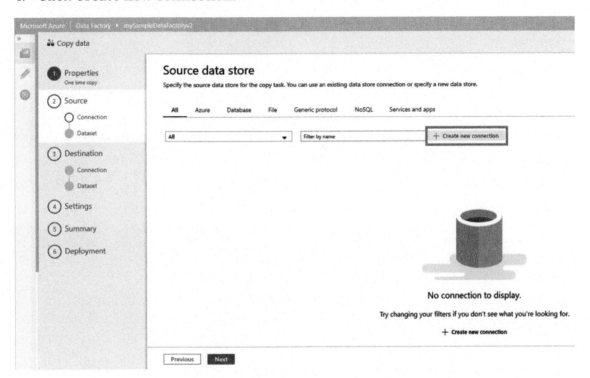

Figure 2.35: Creating a new connection

5. Type **HTTP** in the search box, then click the **HTTP** button from the search result:

Figure 2.36: Selecting the HTTP service

6. Fill in the **New Linked Service (HTTP)** form to define the **Source data store**, as shown in the figure below. For Base URL, enter https://raw.githubusercontent. com/Azure/usql/master/Examples/Samples/Data/json/radiowebsite/small_ radio_json.json

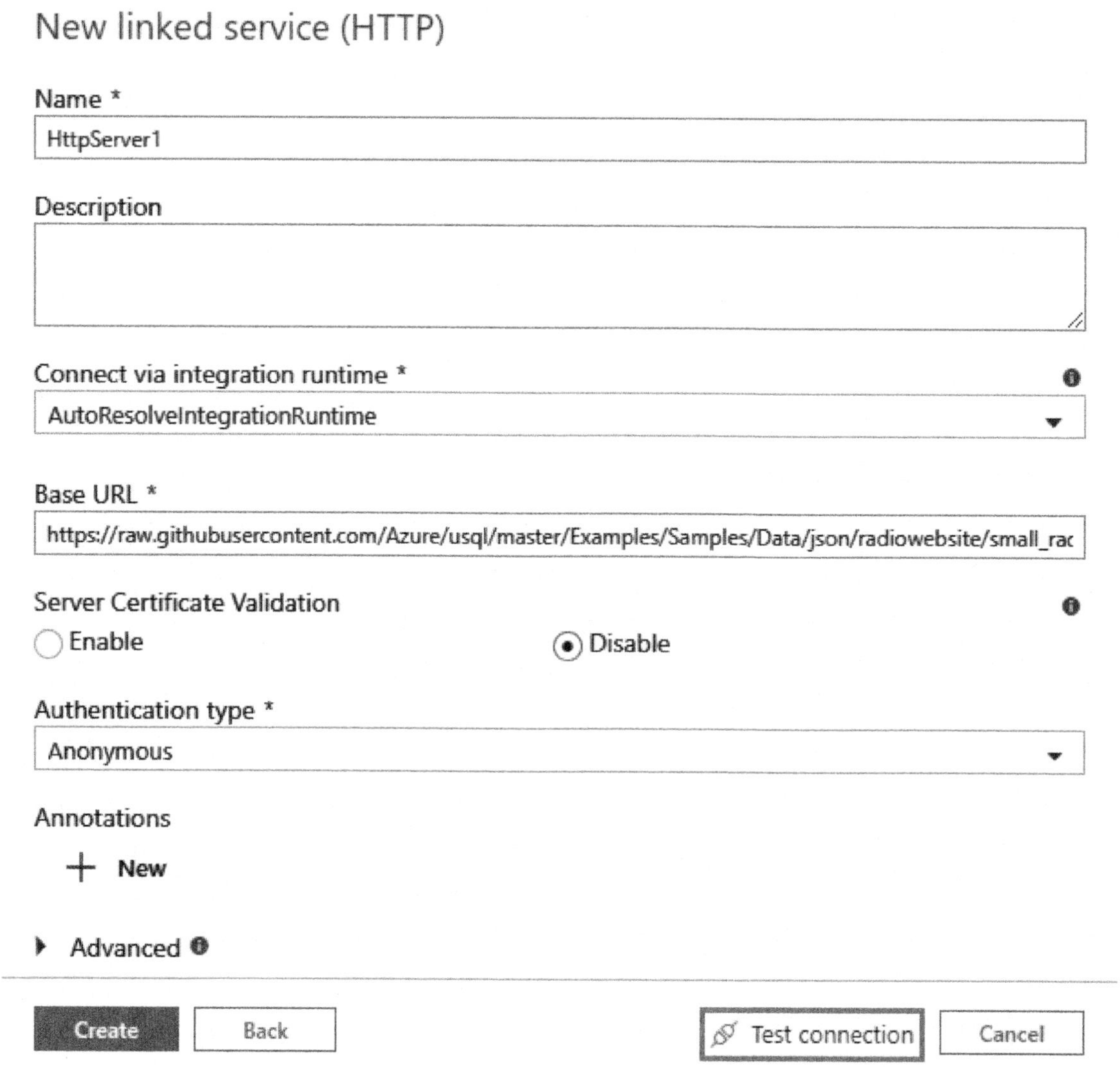

New linked service (HTTP)

Name *

HttpServer1

Description

Connect via integration runtime * ❶

AutoResolveIntegrationRuntime ▼

Base URL *

https://raw.githubusercontent.com/Azure/usql/master/Examples/Samples/Data/json/radiowebsite/small_rac

Server Certificate Validation ❶

◯ Enable   ⦿ Disable

Authentication type *

Anonymous ▼

Annotations

+ New

▸ Advanced ❶

[Create]   [Back]   [✐ Test connection]   [Cancel]

Figure 2.37: Testing new linked service connection

7. If your test connection is successful, click **Create**. Otherwise, make corrections to your entries on this form and test the connection again:

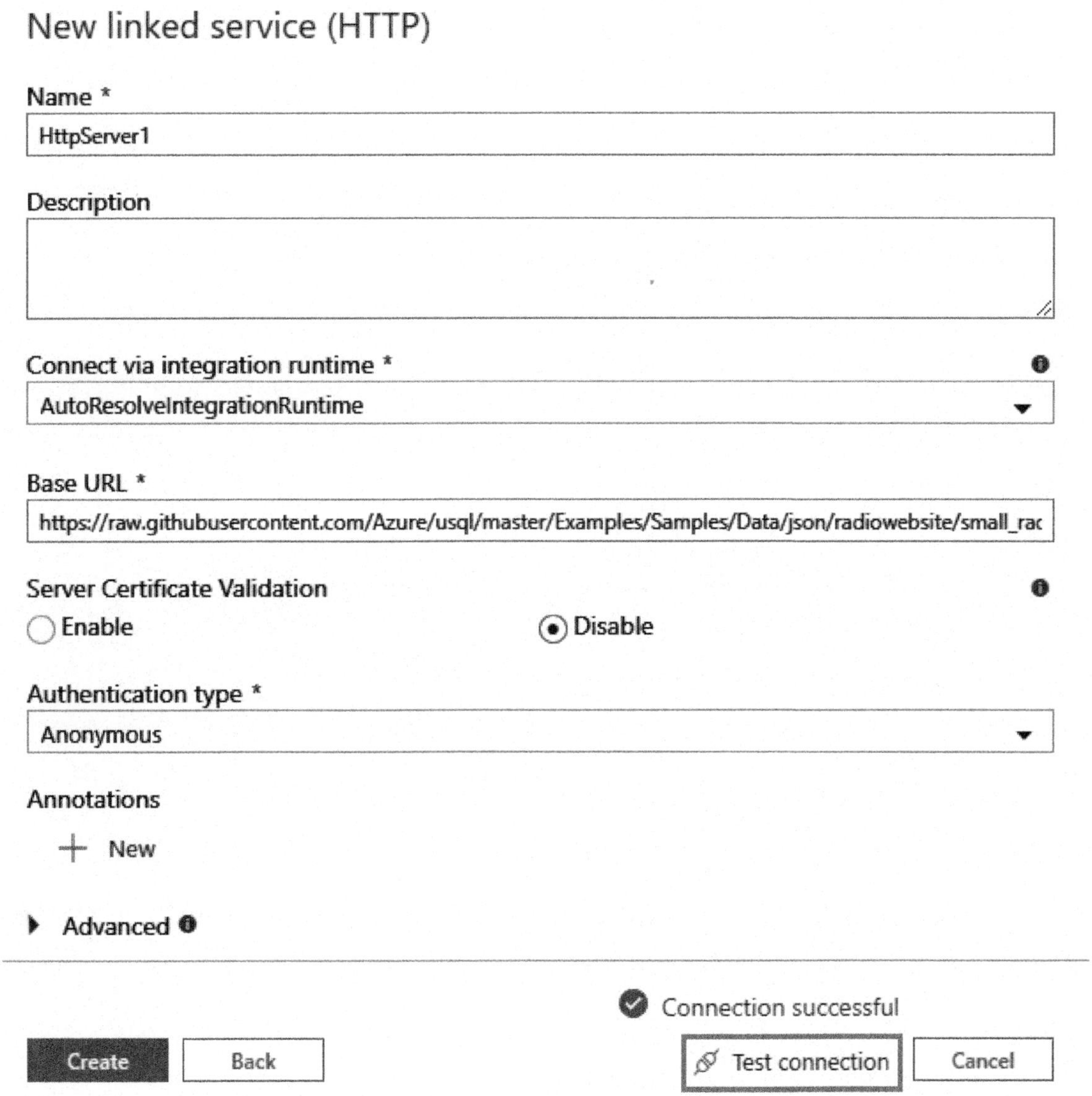

New linked service (HTTP)

Name *

HttpServer1

Description

Connect via integration runtime *   ❶

AutoResolveIntegrationRuntime   ▼

Base URL *

https://raw.githubusercontent.com/Azure/usql/master/Examples/Samples/Data/json/radiowebsite/small_rad

Server Certificate Validation   ❶

◯ Enable   ◉ Disable

Authentication type *

Anonymous   ▼

Annotations

+ New

▶ Advanced ❶

✓ Connection successful

| Create | Back | | 🖉 Test connection | Cancel |

Figure 2.38: Creating HTTP service after successful test connection

8. Click the **Next** button until you reach the File Format settings page:

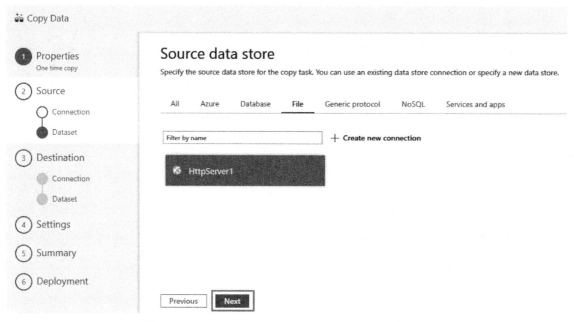

Figure 2.39: Navigating to file format settings page

9. Confirm the **File format settings** as shown in the following figure:

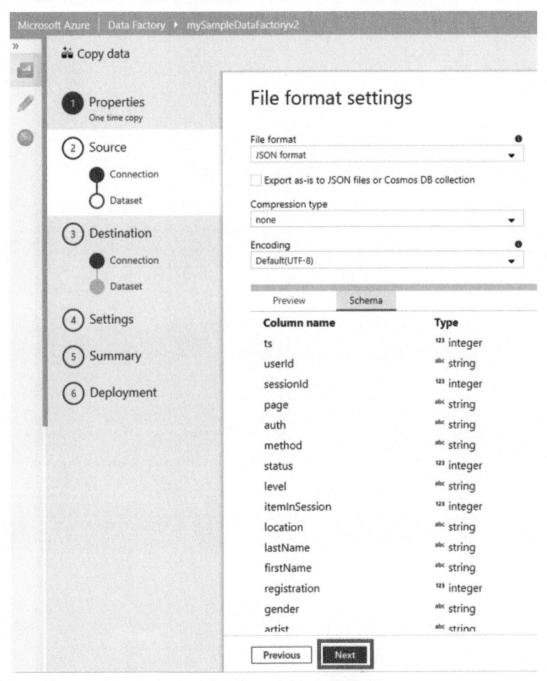

Figure 2.40: File format settings page

The settings can be previewed as follows:

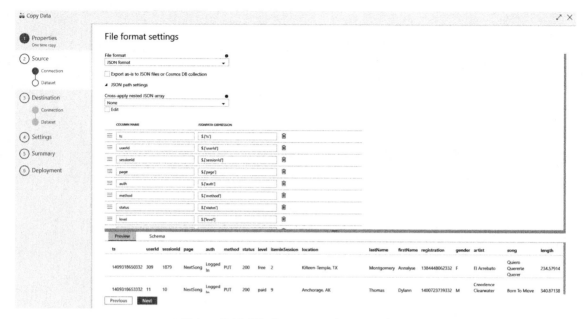

Figure 2.41: File format settings preview

10. Next, click **Create new connection** to configure the **Destination data store**:

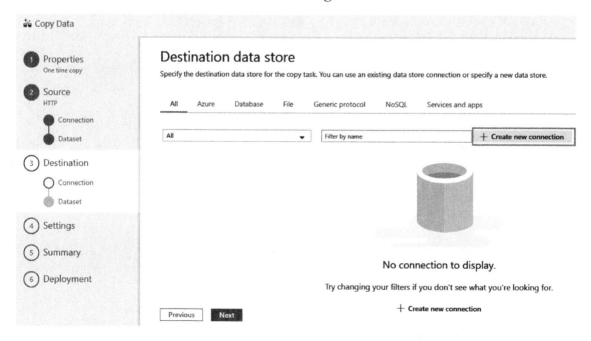

Figure 2.42: Configuring destination data store

11. Select **Azure Data Lake Storage Gen2** and click **Continue**:

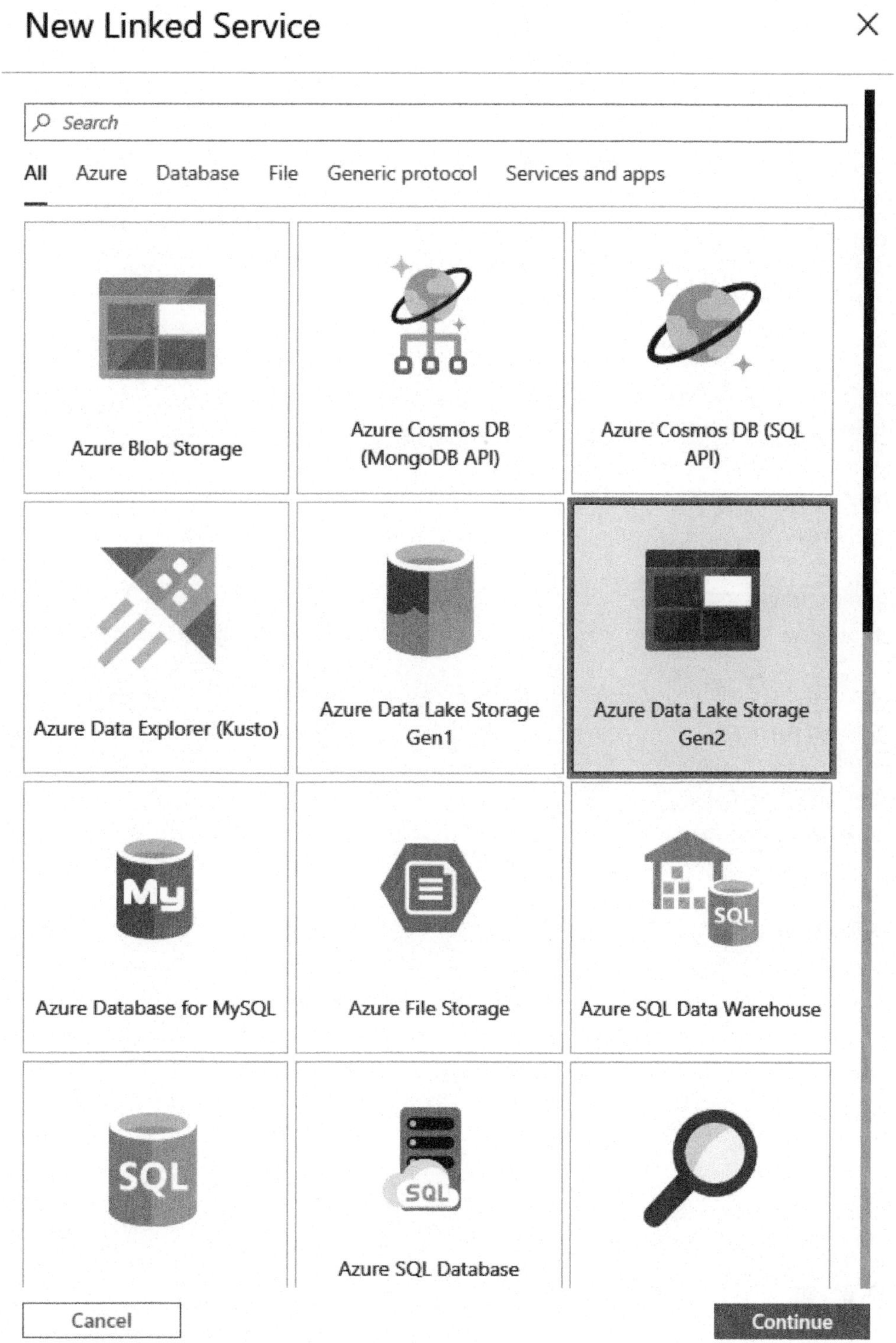

Figure 2.43: Selecting Data Lake Storage Gen2

12. Select the **Azure Data Lake Storage Gen2** (provisioned in the previous exercise), under the **New Linked Service** section:

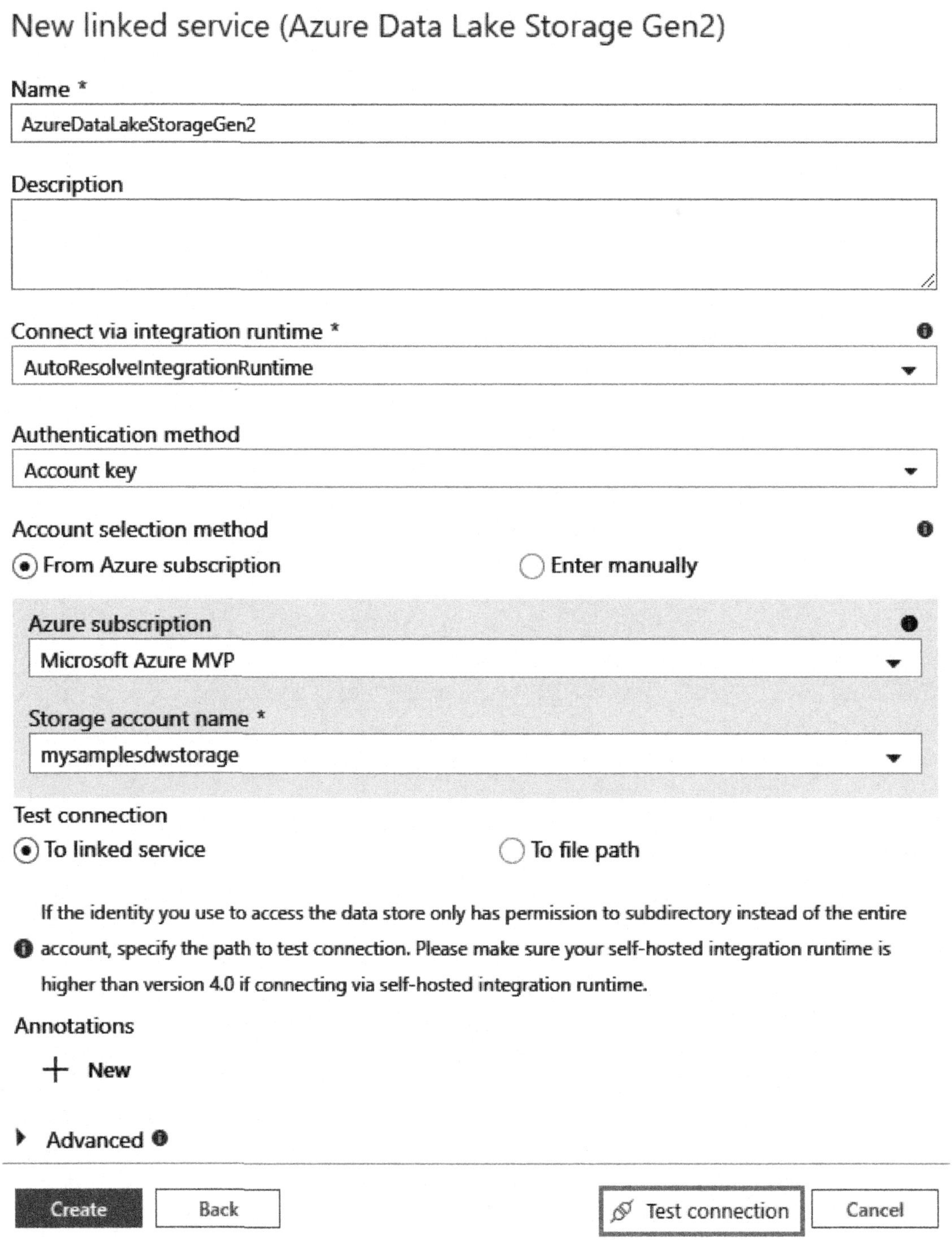

New linked service (Azure Data Lake Storage Gen2)

Name *

AzureDataLakeStorageGen2

Description

Connect via integration runtime *   ❶

AutoResolveIntegrationRuntime   ▼

Authentication method

Account key   ▼

Account selection method   ❶

● From Azure subscription   ○ Enter manually

Azure subscription   ❶

Microsoft Azure MVP   ▼

Storage account name *

mysamplesdwstorage   ▼

Test connection

● To linked service   ○ To file path

❶ If the identity you use to access the data store only has permission to subdirectory instead of the entire account, specify the path to test connection. Please make sure your self-hosted integration runtime is higher than version 4.0 if connecting via self-hosted integration runtime.

Annotations

╋ New

▶ Advanced ❶

───

Create   Back   🖋 Test connection   Cancel

Figure 2.44: Testing connection of provisioned Data Lake Storage

13. If your test connection is successful, click **Create**. Otherwise, make corrections to your entries on the form and test the connection again.

14. Click **Next**:

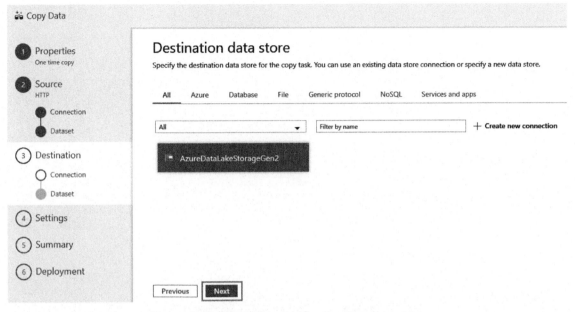

Figure 2.45: Specifying the destination data store

15. Fill out the **Choose the output file or folder** form, as shown in the following figure, and click **Next**:

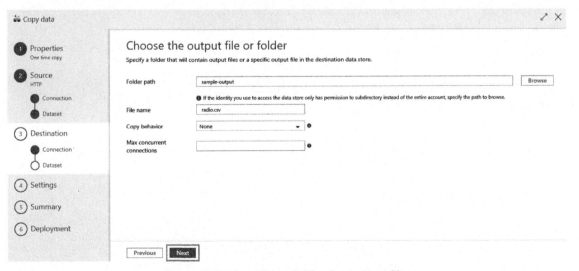

Figure 2.46: Specifying folder for output files

16. Fill out the **File format settings** form, as shown in the following figure, and click **Next**:

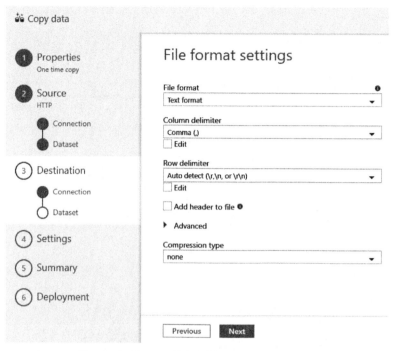

Figure 2.47: Specifying file format settings

17. Accept the default **Schema mapping** and click **Next**:

Figure 2.48: Default Schema mapping

18. Confirm the **Settings** and click **Next**:

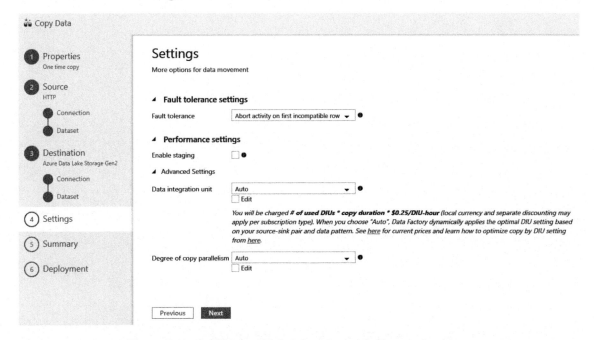

Figure 2.49: Confirming fault tolerance and advanced settings

19. Review the **Summary** and click **Next**:

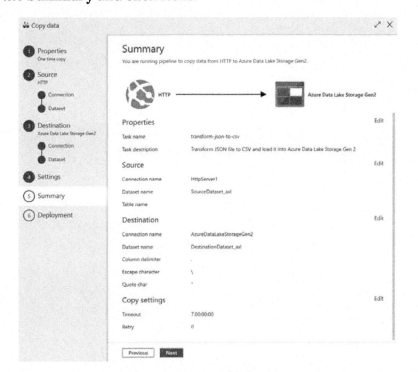

Figure 2.50: Copy data pipeline summary

20. Complete the Deployment by clicking **Finish**:

Figure 2.51: Completing the deployment

Review the result in Azure Data Lake Storage Gen2

At this point, the copy pipeline in Azure Data Factory will have been executed.

1. Go to your Azure Data Lake Storage Gen2 to review the result:

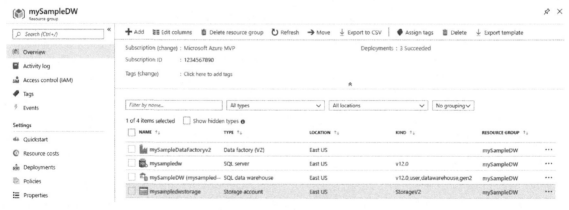

Figure 2.52: Reviewing the result

2. You can use the inbuilt Storage Explorer (preview) to see the resulting file from Azure Data Lake Storage Gen2:

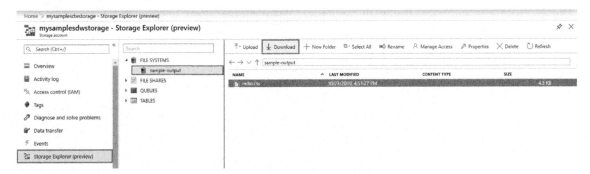

Figure 2.53: Downloading a copy of your csv file

3. Click **Download** to download a copy of **radio.csv** and compare the "before" and "after" versions.

Here is the "before" file in the original JSON format:

Figure 2.54: Original file in JSON format

And here is the transformed file in CSV format that is now stored in Azure Data Lake Storage Gen2:

```
1    1409318650332,"309",1879,"NextSong","Logged In","PUT",200,"free",2,"Killeen-Temple, TX","Montgomery",'
2    1409318653332,"11",10,"NextSong","Logged In","PUT",200,"paid",9,"Anchorage, AK","Thomas","Dylann",140(
3    1409318685332,"201",2047,"NextSong","Logged In","PUT",200,"paid",11,"New York-Newark-Jersey City, NY-I
4    1409318686332,"779",2136,"Home","Logged In","GET",200,"free",0,"Nashville-Davidson--Murfreesboro--Frai
5    1409318697332,"401",400,"NextSong","Logged In","PUT",200,"free",2,"Atlanta-Sandy Springs-Roswell, GA"
6    1409318714332,"521",520,"NextSong","Logged In","PUT",200,"paid",39,"Chicago-Naperville-Elgin, IL-IN-W:
7    1409318743332,"244",2261,"NextSong","Logged In","PUT",200,"free",1,"San Jose-Sunnyvale-Santa Clara, CJ
8    1409318804332,"969",968,"NextSong","Logged In","PUT",200,"paid",0,"Detroit-Warren-Dearborn, MI","Will:
9    1409318832332,"401",400,"NextSong","Logged In","PUT",200,"free",3,"Atlanta-Sandy Springs-Roswell, GA"
10   1409318891332,"779",2136,"NextSong","Logged In","PUT",200,"free",1,"Nashville-Davidson--Murfreesboro--
11   1409318912332,"521",520,"NextSong","Logged In","PUT",200,"paid",40,"Chicago-Naperville-Elgin, IL-IN-W:
12   1409318931332,"201",2047,"NextSong","Logged In","PUT",200,"paid",12,"New York-Newark-Jersey City, NY-I
13   1409318931332,"201",2047,"Home","Logged In","GET",200,"paid",13,"New York-Newark-Jersey City, NY-NJ-PA
```

Figure 2.55: CSV file stored in Azure Data Lake Storage Gen2

At this point, you have built your first Azure Data Factory pipeline to ingest a JSON file, extract the data, transform the data to CSV format, and load the file into Azure Data Lake Storage Gen2.

Provisioning your Azure Databricks Service

Next, we will show you how to provision your Azure Databricks service. Later in the Quick Start Guide, we will complete the modern data warehouse pattern in an exercise which ingests the data in the Azure Data Lake Storage Gen2, prepare the data by cleansing and transforming the data using Azure Databricks, and finally, loading the cleansed and transformed data into the Azure Data Warehouse.

1. Click **Create a resource** in the upper left-hand corner of the Azure Portal:

Figure 2.56: Creating a resource

2. Select **Analytics** under the Azure Marketplace section in **New** page, and choose **Azure Databricks** from the **Featured** section:

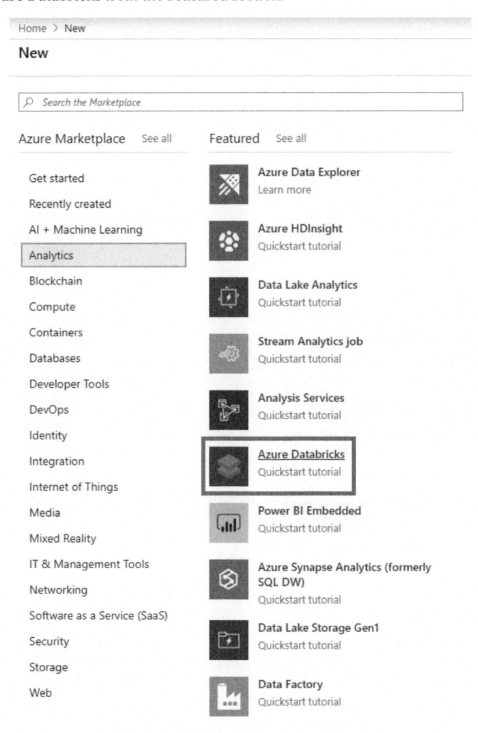

Figure 2.57: Selecting Databricks for provisioning

3. Fill out the **Azure Databricks Service** form as shown in the following figure:

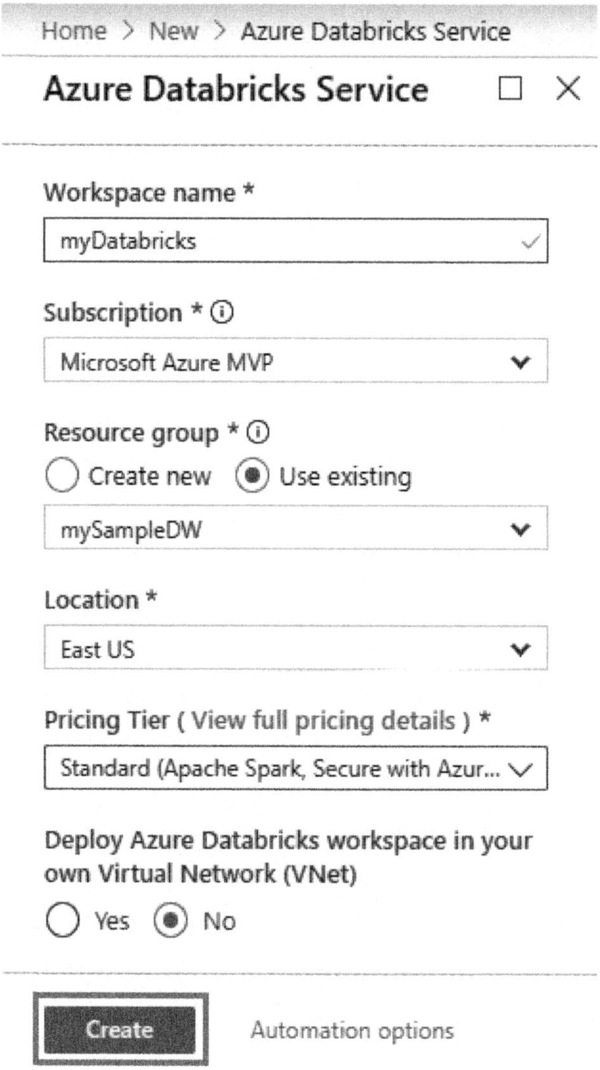

Home > New > Azure Databricks Service

Azure Databricks Service ☐ ✕

Workspace name *

| myDatabricks ✓ |

Subscription * ⓘ

| Microsoft Azure MVP ⌄ |

Resource group * ⓘ
◯ Create new ◉ Use existing

| mySampleDW ⌄ |

Location *

| East US ⌄ |

Pricing Tier (View full pricing details) *

| Standard (Apache Spark, Secure with Azur... ⌄ |

Deploy Azure Databricks workspace in your
own Virtual Network (VNet)
◯ Yes ◉ No

Create   Automation options

Figure 2.58: Adding details to Databricks service

4. Once it is provisioned, select your Azure Databricks service by clicking its name:

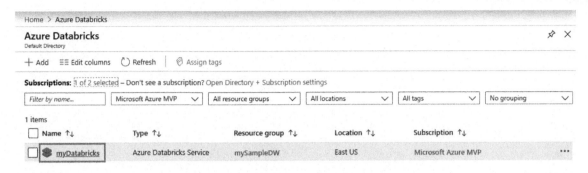

Figure 2.59: Selecting the provisioned Databricks

5. Click **Launch Workspace** to launch the Azure Databricks portal in a separate browser tab:

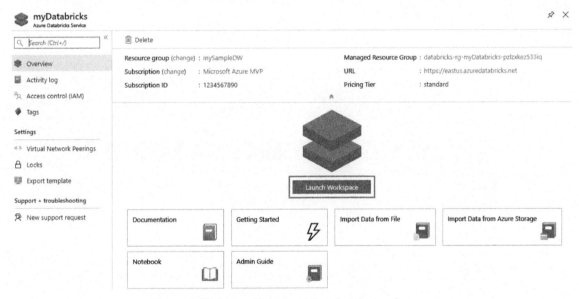

Figure 2.60: Launching your Databricks workspace

6. Next, create a new Spark cluster by clicking **New Cluster**:

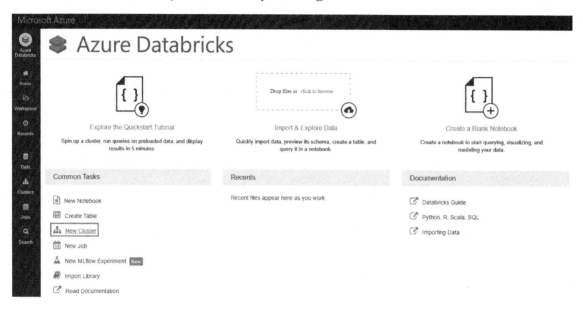

Figure 2.61: Creating a new Spark cluster

7. Fill out the New Cluster page, as shown in the following figure, and click **Create Cluster**:

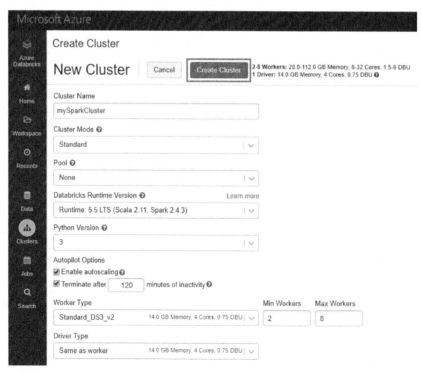

Figure 2.62: Adding details to the Spark cluster

8. Once your Spark cluster is provisioned, you will see a screen similar to this:

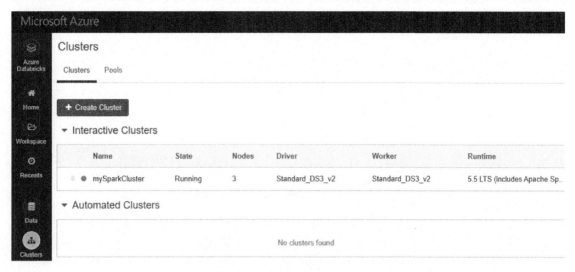

Figure 2.63: Created cluster in running state

You have now provisioned your first Azure Databricks and Spark cluster.

Using Azure Databricks to Prepare and Transform Data

To complete the modern data warehouse process, you need to complete this final exercise. You will ingest data in the Azure Data Lake Storage Gen2, cleanse and transform the data using Azure Databricks, and finally load the cleansed and transformed data in the Azure Synapse Analytics.

1. In the Azure Databricks Workspace, select **Create**, then **Notebook**:

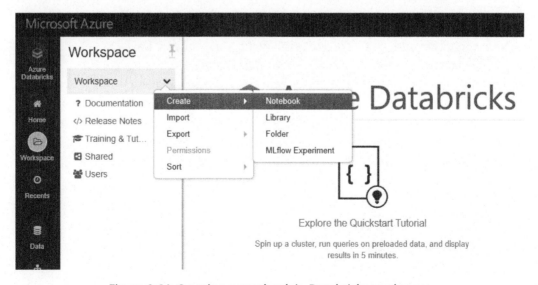

Figure 2.64: Creating a notebook in Databricks workspace

2. Create your Notebook, as shown in the following figure:

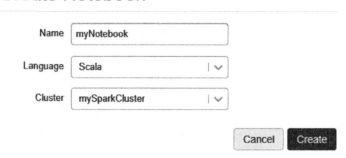

Figure 2.65: Adding details to create the notebook

3. In the first Notebook cell, use the Scala script below to configure your Spark session in your Azure Databricks environment. As indicated in the script, replace the values based on your own environment. Once you have all of your values populated in the script, press *Shift+Enter* to execute the script in the Notebook.

```scala
// replace the following values based on your environment
val storageAccountName = "replace with your own Azure Storage Account
name"
val fileSystemName = "replace with your own File System name"
val tenantID = "replace with your own tenant id"
val appID = "replace with your own appID"
val password = "replace with your own password"
// configuration for blob storage
val blobStorageAcctName = "replace with your own Azure blob storage
account name"
val blobContainer = "replace with your own blob container name"
val blobAccessKey = "replace with your own access key"
// configuration for Azure SQL Data Warehouse
val dwDatabase = "replace with your own database name"
val dwServer = "replace with your own database server name"
val dwUser = "replace with your own database user name"
val dwPass = "replace with your own database password"
val newTable = "replace with your own new table name"
```

Note

For the Scala script that follows, enter each code block in your Azure Databricks Notebook cell, and press *Shift+Enter* to execute each code block. Observe your results after each execution.

4. Configure Spark session as follows:

```
spark.conf.set("fs.azure.account.auth.type", "OAuth")
spark.conf.set("fs.azure.account.oauth.provider.type", "org.apache.hadoop.
fs.azurebfs.oauth2.ClientCredsTokenProvider")
spark.conf.set("fs.azure.account.oauth2.client.id", "" + appID + "")
spark.conf.set("fs.azure.account.oauth2.client.secret", "" + password +
"")
spark.conf.set("fs.azure.account.oauth2.client.endpoint", "https://login.
microsoftonline.com/" + tenantID + "/oauth2/token")
spark.conf.set("fs.azure.createRemoteFileSystemDuringInitialization",
"true")
dbutils.fs.ls("abfss://" + fileSystemName + "@" + storageAccountName +
".dfs.core.windows.net/")
spark.conf.set("fs.azure.createRemoteFileSystemDuringInitialization",
"false")
```

5. Configure Azure Data Lake Storage Gen2 account as follows:

```
spark.conf.set("fs.azure.account.auth.type." + storageAccountName + ".dfs.
core.windows.net", "OAuth")
spark.conf.set("fs.azure.account.oauth.provider.type." +
storageAccountName + ".dfs.core.windows.net", "org.apache.hadoop.
fs.azurebfs.oauth2.ClientCredsTokenProvider")
spark.conf.set("fs.azure.account.oauth2.client.id." + storageAccountName +
".dfs.core.windows.net", "" + appID + "")
spark.conf.set("fs.azure.account.oauth2.client.secret." +
storageAccountName + ".dfs.core.windows.net", "" + password + "")
spark.conf.set("fs.azure.account.oauth2.client.endpoint." +
storageAccountName + ".dfs.core.windows.net", "https://login.
microsoftonline.com/" + tenantID + "/oauth2/token")
spark.conf.set("fs.azure.createRemoteFileSystemDuringInitialization",
"true")
dbutils.fs.ls("abfss://" + fileSystemName + "@" + storageAccountName +
".dfs.core.windows.net/")
spark.conf.set("fs.azure.createRemoteFileSystemDuringInitialization",
"false")
```

6. Fetch the sample JSON file into **/tmp** as follows:

```
%sh wget -P /tmp https://raw.githubusercontent.com/Azure/usql/master/
Examples/Samples/Data/json/radiowebsite/small_radio_json.json
```

7. Copy the sample file from **/tmp** to Azure Data Lake Storage Gen2:

```
dbutils.fs.cp("file:///tmp/sample.json", "abfss://" + fileSystemName + "@" +
storageAccountName + ".dfs.core.windows.net/")
```

8. Load the sample JSON file into a DataFrame:

```
val df = spark.read.json("abfss://" + fileSystemName + "@" +
storageAccountName + ".dfs.core.windows.net/sample.json")
```

9. Output the contents of the DataFrame to ensure everything is working properly:

```
df.show()
```

10. Cleanse the data by selecting only two columns:

```
// called firstName and lastName from the DataFrame
val specificColumnsDf = df.select("firstname", "lastname")
```

11. Output the selection results:

```
specificColumnsDf.show()
```

12. Transform the data by renaming the **lastName** column to **surname**:

```
val transformedDF = specificColumnsDf.withColumnRenamed("lastName",
"surname")
```

13. Output the transformed results:

```
transformedDF.show()
```

14. Load the data into Azure SQL Data Warehouse:

```
val blobStorage = blobStorageAcctName + ".blob.core.windows.net"
val tempDir = "wasbs://" + blobContainer + "@" + blobStorage + "/tempdir"
val acntInfo = "fs.azure.account.key." + blobStorage
sc.hadoopConfiguration.set(acntInfo, blobAccessKey)
```

15. Load the transformed **DataFrame** in Azure SQL Data Warehouse as a new table called **NewTable**:

```
val dwJdbcPort = "1433"
val dwJdbcExtraOptions =
"encrypt=true;trustServerCertificate=true;hostNameInCertificate=*.database.
windows.net;loginTimeout=30;"
val sqlDwUrl = "jdbc:sqlserver://" + dwServer + ":" + dwJdbcPort +
";database=" + dwDatabase + ";user=" + dwUser+";password=" + dwPass +
";$dwJdbcExtraOptions"
val sqlDwUrlSmall = "jdbc:sqlserver://" + dwServer + ":" + dwJdbcPort +
";database=" + dwDatabase + ";user=" + dwUser+";password=" + dwPass
spark.conf.set("spark.sql.parquet.writeLegacyFormat", "true")
transformedDF.write.format("com.databricks.spark.sqldw").option("url",
sqlDwUrlSmall).option("dbtable", newTable).option("forward_spark_azure_
storage_credentials","True").option("tempdir", tempDir).mode("overwrite").
save()
```

In completing the execution of each of the code blocks above, you will have ingested a sample JSON file into Azure Data Lake Storage Gen2, cleansed the data by selecting only the two desired columns, transformed one column name from **lastName** to **surname**, and loaded the transformed **DataFrame** into Azure Synapse Analytics. This completes the entire modern data warehouse process.

Clean Up Your Azure Synapse Analytics

If you no longer need to use your Azure Synapse Analytics (formerly SQL DW), you can save money by permanently deleting its resource group. In this approach, you will permanently delete the Azure Synapse Analytics (formerly SQL DW) and all associated resources (e.g. Azure Data Factory, Azure Data Lake Storage Gen2, Azure Databricks, etc.) which you have provisioned within the same resource group. This can be done by navigating to the overview pane and clicking **Delete resource group**, as shown in the following figure:

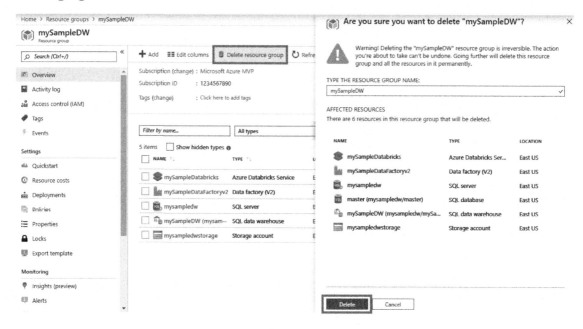

Figure 2.66: Cleaning your data warehouse by deleting resource group

Summary

In this chapter, you have closely studied Azure Synapse Analytics, Azure Data Lake Storage Gen2, Azure Data Factory, and Azure Databricks. You learned about the features and benefits of each of these key technologies, as well as how to provision your own Azure Synapse Analytics (formerly SQL DW). The next chapter will focus on the analytical side of the modern data warehouse. It will demonstrate how you can process and visualize the data using Power BI, and also implement machine learning. Later in the book, you will see real use cases on how all of these technologies integrate with one another to provide the complete end-to-end data warehouse solutions business decision-makers can use to derive meaningful insights from real-time data.

3

Processing and Visualizing Data

In the last chapter, we provisioned Azure Data Factory, Azure Data Lake Storage, and Azure Synapse Analytics (formerly known as Azure SQL Data Warehouse) to ingest and store data. We also transformed unstructured data into a structured format with the help of Azure Databricks.

In this chapter, we will analyze our structured data to gain meaningful insights. This chapter will be divided into two main parts:

- Data Modeling and serving using Azure Analysis Services
- Data Visualization using Power BI

Azure Analysis Services

Businesses are constantly generating vast amounts of data in various formats from multiple sources. However, these businesses often have difficulty in ensuring every stakeholder can access it because of complex infrastructure that limits them to get timely access to relevant data. Real-time access to data is key to have a seamless data-driven culture. Often, Analysts and Data scientists cannot directly explore and analyze the data sets from their company's databases for the following reasons:

- Confidential information might be leaked.

- Performing analysis directly to the production servers can affect performance and might contribute to down time.

Semantic data modeling is a phase where you want to create a semantic data model so that analysts can have seamless access to data. A semantic data model is a tabular format that is structured and can easily be visualized and understood by most users. In practice, analysts do not query transactional databases directly because these databases are meant for the actual end customers and applications; instead they build a data model and store it to the data warehouse. Often the semantic model data is just a cached version of the production data and will eventually be deleted or refreshed. Azure Analysis Services can bridge this data gap.

Azure Analysis Services (AAS) is a cloud hosted service and a fully managed platform as a service (PaaS) tool that enables data engineers to model database tables and serve these semantic data models to users. An example is generating sales reports where you have multiple sources of data and the stakeholders would just want to know if the company is earning or losing money. These data models provide a seamless way for users (specifically analysts) to explore and browse massive amounts of cached data for on demand data analysis. This ensures that analysts do not have to wait for data engineers to manually create a snapshot of the data (often in CSV or Excel format) and then data engineers send it over to analysts via email.

SQL Server Analysis Services

Given the inherited features of AAS from SSAS (SQL Server Analysis Services), it would be easier to explain first the capabilities of SSAS to further understand the connection points between a data source and Power BI.

The following diagram shows a hybrid architecture using SSAS to analyze data and connect through Power BI service via VPN Gateway:

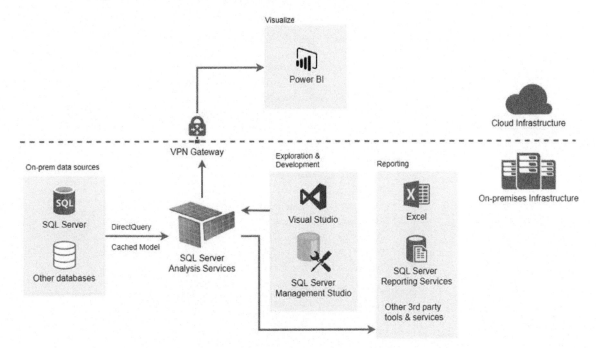

Figure 3.1: SQL Server Analysis Services

In an on-premises scenario, your database (or data warehouse) is hosted on your own datacenter. SQL Server Analysis Services is typically used by organizations today for their on-premises BI solution. It allows data engineers to connect to their on-premise data sources and turn complex datasets into a single structured database commonly referred to as SSOT (single source of truth).

Data engineers use tools like Visual Studio or SQL Server Management Studio (SSMS) to author, explore, and develop semantic data models that they can eventually send either as a report or as tabular models for Power BI (or other business intelligence tools).

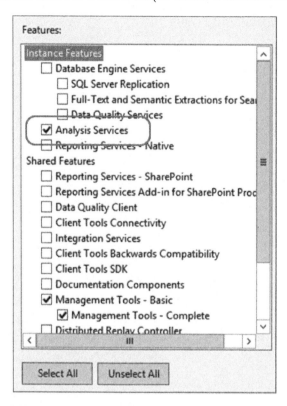

Figure 3.2: Analysis Services listed in Features window

The biggest caveat with semantic data modeling in SQL Server Analysis Services is the high dependency on the SQL Server instance and licensing. Given that your data center is on premises, scaling on-demand will be a challenge. That's where Azure Analysis Services shines over SSAS.

AAS is a cloud-hosted service that is easily scalable and independent of a SQL Server instance. Below are some of the main features and benefits of using AAS.

Features and Benefits

Azure Analysis Services is built on the proven analytical engine of SQL Server 2016 Analysis Services. It runs analysis services natively on cloud resources such as Azure Synapse Analytics.

AAS offers the following features:

- The user can combine data from different complex sources and create a tabular representation of data that is easily understood by most people.

- The platform provides on-demand performance that can match the scale of your data size and operations.

- AAS also provides an added layer of security that ensures only the right people get access to the right set of data (role-based access control) using Azure Active Directory.

Azure Analysis Services is easy to deploy, scale, and manage as it is a PAAS solution. You can provision an Azure Analysis Service within seconds. You have the elasticity to scale your operation tiers up or down depending on how frequently you need the service. Lastly, it removes the burden of managing the underlying infrastructure (such as Networking, Disk Spaces, Memory, and Hard Drives) since it is fully managed in the cloud.

Figure 3.3 depicts the revised architecture once you move from SSAS to AAS:

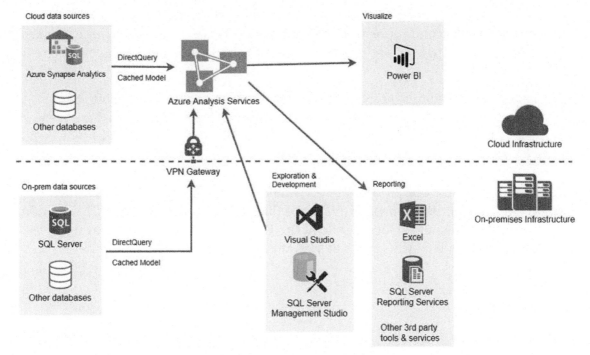

Figure 3.3: Azure Analysis Services

In the preceding diagram, AAS acts as the bridge between Azure Synapse Analytics (used to store data) and Power BI which serves as a visualization tool. This does not mean that AAS is only limited to using Azure Synapse Analytics as a data source. AAS can connect with several on-premises and cloud database solutions.

Azure Analysis Services has all the same functionalities and capabilities as SQL Server Analysis Services, but it is a fully-managed cloud service. AAS supports complex model scenarios such as bi-directional cross filters. An example of this is creating meaningful insights from customers and products who have a many-to-many data relationship, where a customer can buy multiple products and the same product can be bought by different customers.

AAS is highly scalable. It can scale linearly by increasing the number of cores, and can also use the Intel TBB-based (Threading Building Blocks) scalable allocator that provides separate memory pools for every core.

Power BI

Power BI is a suite of tools that lets users visualize data and share insights across teams and organizations, or embed in their websites or applications. It supports different data sources (both structured and unstructured data types.) It helps analysts and end-users create live dashboards and reports about the business' data on-demand. An example of this is visualizing company sales for the past months and determining the city that sold the most items.

What makes Power BI different from a spreadsheet software like Microsoft Excel is that it is designed to be a hosted user interface (often a live dashboard) where users don't need to frequently store a file in their local machine and open it. With Power BI, you can leverage the power of the cloud to harness complex data and represent them through rich graphs or charts, letting the server run all the computations, rather than your own machine. In a scenario where your data size was to grow from 500 megabytes to gigabytes, most general-purpose machines (like personal computers with a limited amount of memory) would struggle to load the Excel file; however, with Power BI, it is just like opening a web page as it is a hosted service.

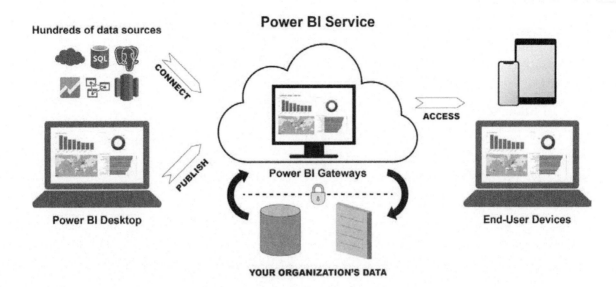

Figure 3.4: Power BI Architecture

Power BI is composed of different components that can perform different functions:

Power BI Desktop

This is a Windows desktop-based application that is often referred to as an "Authoring Tool" where you primarily design and publish reports to the service.

Power BI

This is the managed platform to deploy your reports. It is a Software as a service (SaaS) application and has evolved from "Power BI for Office 365" to just Power BI.

Power BI Mobile Apps

These are native mobile applications that can access reports from a workspace that is hosted in Power BI. It is available on the Apple iOS App Store and Google Play Store.

Power BI Gateway

Gateway is a mechanism to sync external data into Power BI. For enterprise scenarios with on-premises storage, Power BI Gateway acts as a mechanism to query against the data source without the need to transfer databases to the cloud. However, the data that is hosted in Power BI reports lives within Azure Cloud.

Power BI Report Server

In an on-premises scenario, Power BI Report Server allows you to host Power BI reports within your own data center. These reports are still share-able across different members, as long as they have the right network access.

Power BI Embedded

Embedded allows you to white label Power BI in your own custom applications. Strategically these are often integrated into existing dashboards and back-office systems where the same set of users can only access the reports.

Features and Benefits

On a high level, Power BI offers the following benefits:

- Personalized dashboards that allow analysts to brand the look and feel of the graphs, charts, and tables.

- Collaboration across different users.

- Governance and security that ensures that only authorized users can access the dashboards.

- No memory or speed constraints, as it is a cloud-hosted service. It is as if the user is just loading a web page.

- No specialized technical support is required, as reports are meant to be easy to interact with.

- Support for advanced data services, such as the "Ask a Question" feature, integration with R, segmentation and cohort analysis.

Power BI is an intuitive tool that often just requires clicking or drag-and-dropping in order to quickly access and visualize data. The authoring tool (Power BI Desktop) is equipped with many built-in features to derive analytics. It is smart enough to suggest a visualization model based on the fields of your choice.

Power BI Dashboards and Reports are highly customizable and allow you to personalize the experience depending on your branding. You can select themes, use custom charts, create labels, insert drawings and images, and a lot more.

Compared to sending an email with a PowerPoint file attached, Power BI allows an open collaboration between analysts and other members of the company just by sharing a centralized dashboard. You can access the reports using major web browsers or by means of mobile applications that you can download in the Apple App Store and Google Play Store. People can send comments and annotations about the reports, creating a faster feedback loop with the use of alerts and notifications.

Power BI is secure in different facets and areas. For one, when authoring a report, you are ensured that you can only access data sources that you have access to. This is backed by **Row Level Security** (**RLS**). For example, analysts can only access data that is local to their region, making sure they don't have access to another city or country's data. Once you are ready to share the report, you can quickly save it to your personal workspace. You can select whomever you want to share the report with across your organization, or invite users from external tenants.

If you wish to start small while learning Power BI, you can start with just using Excel files as your data source. There are scenarios where analysts receive a CSV file from data engineers because the size of the data set is not too large.

In this book, we will use Power BI to generate reports from semantic data models of AAS. Although Power BI supports multiple data sources, including Azure Synapse Analytics and on-premises databases, it is best practice to consume an Analysis Service instead. Sometimes you can also query from a cached result of Azure Databricks.

There are different approaches to this, but the major reason for using this approach (AAS + Power BI as shown in *Figure 3.3*) is mainly around elasticity and separation of duties. If you are using AAS, you get a snapshot of the state of your data sources all the way from IoT streams and databases (with the help of ADF, Data Lake, SQL DW). The data from your production transactional database is cached and would not create a significant impact on the performance, even if you have billions of rows in your databases.

Quick Start Guide (Data Modeling and Visualization)

Now that we understand AAS and Power BI, we will proceed with data modeling and visualization using these tools/services.

Prerequisites

In order to perform this activity, you need the following:

- An active Azure Subscription
- Power BI Desktop
- Authoring tool (Optional)
- SQL Server Data Tools (SSDT) on Visual Studio
- SQL Server Management Studio
- Azure Synapse Analytics as AAS Data source (optional)

Provisioning the Azure Analysis Service

In the Azure portal, search for **Analysis Services** and click on the Create button.

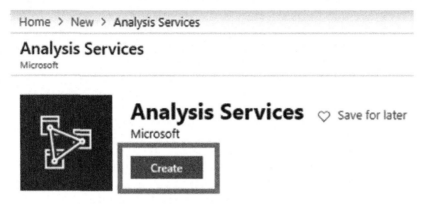

Figure 3.5: Creating an Azure Analysis service

In Analysis Services, fill in the required fields, and then press Create:

- **Server name**: A unique name for the resource.

- **Subscription**: A subscription where you want to provision your resource.

- **Resource group**: A logical grouping of resources for centralized management of access controls, locks, and tags.

- **Location**: The datacenter region to host the server.

- **Pricing tier**: For development purposes, you can choose D1.

- **Administrator**: A privileged user of the server. You can add more later on.

- **Backup Storage settings**: Optional. Storage for model database backup.

- **Storage key expiration**: Optional. Specify the time period for which the storage key can be used.

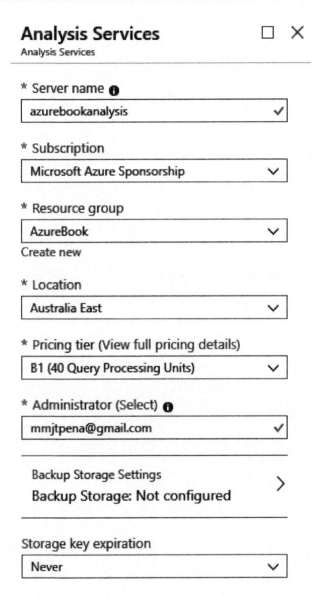

Figure 3.6: Adding details to the Analysis service

Provisioning the server usually does not take longer than a minute.

Allowing Client Access

When authoring a semantic data model, you need to use a desktop tool such as Power BI Desktop, SQL Server Data Tools (SSDT) for Visual Studio, or SQL Server Management Studio (SSMS). Since the server is hosted on the cloud, you need to whitelist your IP Address in order for your client app (SSDT or SSMS) to have access to the Azure Analysis Services server.

1. In the provisioned Analysis Services, go to the **Firewall** section. (Refer to *figure* 3.7)

2. Ensure that the firewall is enabled so that your server is not publicly available to be accessed.

3. Click on **Allow access from Power BI** so that Power BI service can perform a `DirectQuery` access.

4. Click on **Add Client IP**. This will add your existing client's IP to the whitelisted IPs.

   Optionally, you can specify an IP address range that you wish to allow access.

5. Click **Save**.

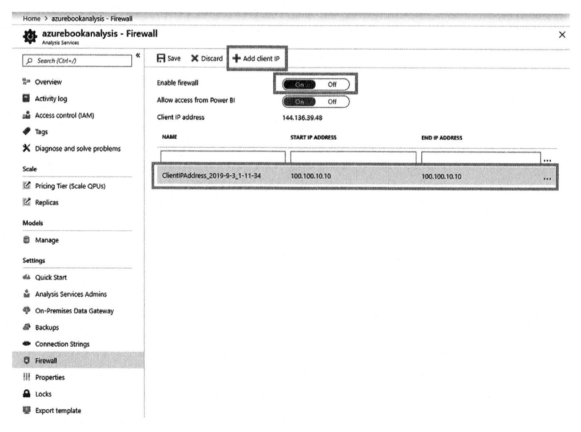

Figure 3.7: Enabling firewall access to Power BI

By performing this activity, your client machine (such as a laptop) now has access to the AAS models. This is a very powerful feature of Azure that allows only certain IP addresses to have access to its service.

Creating a Model

In this section we will create a model by performing the following steps:

1. In the same Analysis Services resource, go to the **Manage** tab under the **Models** section.

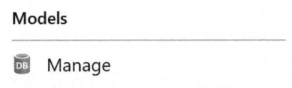

Figure 3.8: Creating a new model

2. Click on the **New model** button and a blade will appear. For the simplicity of this exercise, choose **Sample data** and click **Add**.

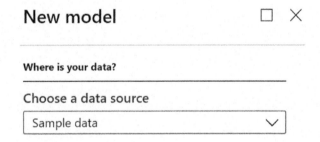

Figure 3.9: Choosing the sample data as AAS data source

> **Note**
>
> This will create a new deployed semantic model to your AAS based from the famous **AdventureWorks** database with online retail bike stores data.

In practice, you will use an authoring tool like SQL Server Development Tools on Visual Studio and build a tabular model on top of your Azure Synapse Analytics. This is done by creating an Analysis Services Tabular Project from Visual Studio.

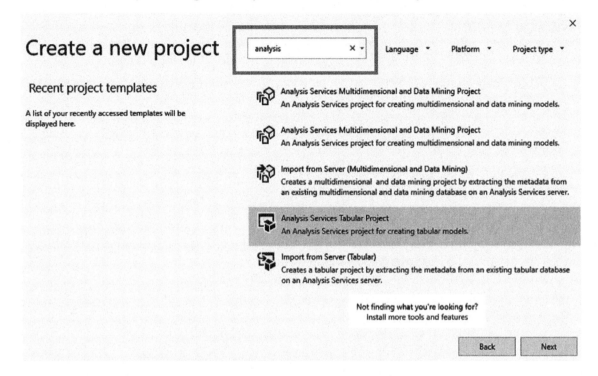

Figure 3.10: SQL Server Development Tools on Visual Studio

We did not go in-depth by creating a data model in this book, but if you're interested in learning more, Microsoft has created a handy resource in creating an Analysis Services data model with 1400 Compatibility. 1400 means that it works for both Azure Analysis Services and SQL Server Analysis Services.

You can read more about this at https://packt.live/35ekZoL.

Download Resources:

- Visual Studio (https://packt.live/32YG3hu)
- SSDT (https://packt.live/37hUhNY)
- SSMS (https://packt.live/333wzBv)

Opening the Created Model with Power BI

In this section, we will open the created model in Power BI Desktop.

After creating a model, make sure you stay on the Manage model tab. Click on the ellipsis available at the right-hand portion of the model and then click **Open in Power BI Desktop**.

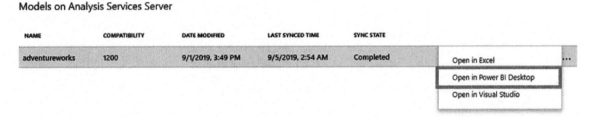

Models on Analysis Services Server

NAME	COMPATIBILITY	DATE MODIFIED	LAST SYNCED TIME	SYNC STATE	
adventureworks	1200	9/1/2019, 3:49 PM	9/5/2019, 2:54 AM	Completed	Open in Excel ···
					Open in Power BI Desktop
					Open in Visual Studio

Figure 3.11: Opening Power BI Desktop

AAS will then download a `.pbix` file which is a Power BI Desktop file where a connection between the `AdventureWorks` data model and Power BI has been established.

In the following parts of the activity, you will need to use Power BI Desktop to create a live dashboard.

As of writing, Power BI Desktop has the following limitations:

- It only works on Windows 7 / Windows Server 2008 R2, or later

- You need to use a work email address in order to create reports and dashboards using Power BI Desktop. However, guest access can be given to a consumer email address (like `@outlook.com` or `@gmail.com`) to view the reports and dashboards from Power BI service.

> **Note**
>
> If you haven't downloaded Power BI Desktop, you can download it for free from the Microsoft Store app for Windows 10 or download the standalone installer at https://packt.live/2KCILmG. To get started with Power BI Desktop, use a work email address to register. Go to the following link in order to check if you are eligible to create an account (https://packt.live/2Oqw2Ve).

In an enterprise scenario, you will use the same work account when accessing the Azure portal. Since they are on the same Azure Active Directory tenant, some access control levels will be inherited. If you used a personal account for your Azure portal and a separate work email for your Power BI account, then you need to add the account associated with Power BI into the Azure Analysis Server as admin.

Perform the following steps to open the model in Power BI:

1.   Go back to the Azure portal. In the same Azure Analysis Services resource, go to **Analysis Services Admins**.

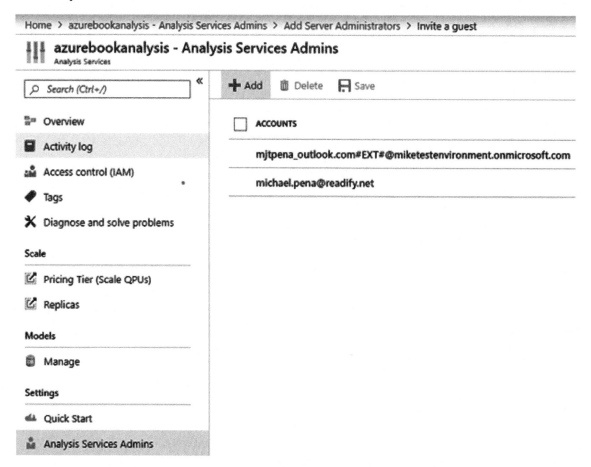

Figure 3.12: Adding a guest admin

2. Click on **Add**.

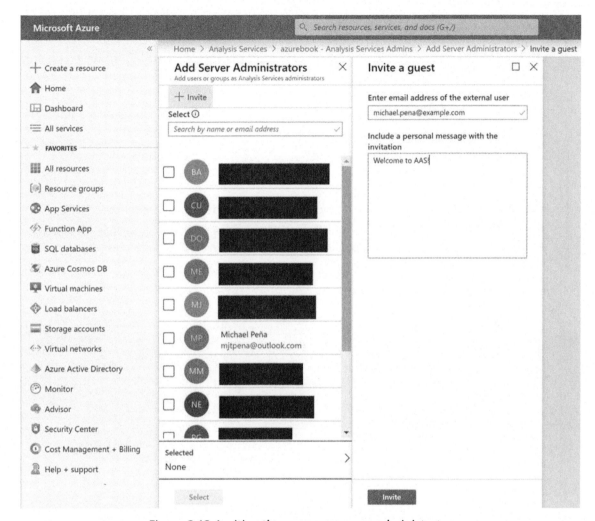

Figure 3.13: Inviting the user as a server administrator

Either add a user from the same Active Directory / tenant or invite a guest user from a different tenant. Add the email address associated when you created a Power BI account.

3. After you have completed downloading Power BI Desktop, creating a Power BI account, and allowing admin access to Azure Analysis Services server, click on the `.pbix` file you previously downloaded from AAS.

4. It will open the Power BI Desktop app and may prompt you to log-in. Use the same credentials that were used to create a Power BI account from the previous steps. If you encountered an error while opening the file, one probable reason is that the account you used to login to Power BI is not an admin of the Azure Analysis Services, hence it cannot create a connection.

> **Note**
>
> Note that you don't need Azure Analysis Services in order to create a Power BI report. Power BI supports different data sources such as Azure Synapse Analytics directly, although it is not recommended for production and real-life use.

5. After opening the file, make sure you see fields on the right-hand side of the desktop app.

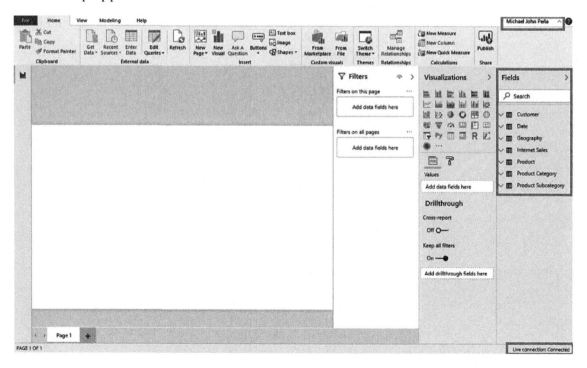

Figure 3.14: Field section of the selected database

These fields indicate that you have an active connection to Azure Analysis Services, as you can now query against the semantic data model.

You are now ready to proceed to the next part of the activity, which is creating the live dashboard.

Visualizing Data

Now that you have available fields to play around, it's time to generate insights from the data. In an enterprise scenario, using AAS as your Power BI data source gives you the flexibility to query against a cached model from your Azure Synapse Analytics where you have all the required access to the data as an analyst. You would not need to wait for a database administrator or engineer to send you a .csv file to start visualizing the data. In theory, the data that you are about to build reports around reflects a snapshot of your existing databases. In this particular scenario, AdventureWorks may derive this data from multiple data sources such as databases, storage, IoT sensors, and social media. It is not a best practice for Power BI to query directly against those data sources.

Power BI is a very intuitive tool, and most of the steps just require drag-and-drops and clicks. Using the AdventureWorks database as our data source for AAS, we will see fields that are related to an online retail store selling bikes and associated equipment. It has pre-populated fields for you, but in general, the fields have the following meanings:

- **Internet Sales**: Sales data associated with the products
- **Product**: Metadata for the product, such as its name
- **Product Category**: A high-level category association of the products
- **Product Subcategory**: A lower-level categorization of the products
- **Customer**: Customer-related information about the sale of a product
- **Date**: A measure of time for the sales of the products
- **Geography**: A measure of location for the sales of the products

We'll now perform the following steps to visualize the data in Power BI:

1. Let us start with a simple **Product Category** table that shows product names. On the **fields** section of the app, click on the **Product Category** table, and select **Product Category Name**:

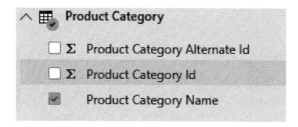

Figure 3.15: Product Category table

This will create a table that looks like this:

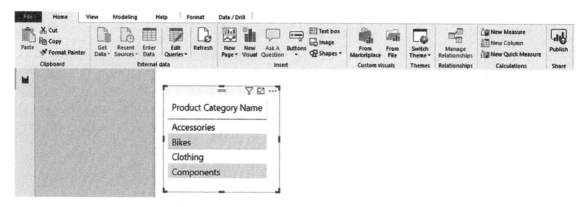

Figure 3.16: Product Category Name table

As you can see, Power BI is interactive and smart enough to display a table to represent the list of category names.

2. Next we will display a similar table for product subcategories. Similar to the **Categories** field, go to the **Product Subcategory** field and click on **Product Subcategory Name**. This will create another table that lists all subcategories.

The interesting point to note here is that given the two tables, Power BI is smart enough to highlight correlations between the two.

3. In the **Product Category Name** table, click on the **Bikes** row:

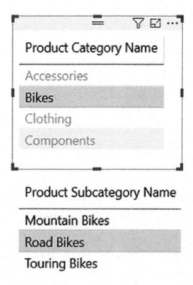

Figure 3.17: Power BI filtering product subcategories

As you can see, Power BI automatically filters all the product subcategories that belong to the parent category. It displays **Mountain Bikes**, **Road Bikes**, and **Touring Bikes**, which are all associated with the **Bikes** product category. Ideally this is something you (or the database engineer/administrator) set in your semantic data model in Analysis Services.

4. If you click on the same "**Bikes**" row from the **Product Category Name** again, it will remove the filter of the subcategories.

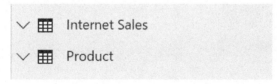

Figure 3.18: Internet Sales and Product Fields

5. Let us now create another table that associates **Internet Sales** and **Product**. In the **Internet Sales** field, click on **Internet Total Sales** and in the **Product** field, click on **Category**. Power BI will automatically create a clustered column chart for you as shown in *Figure 3.19*:

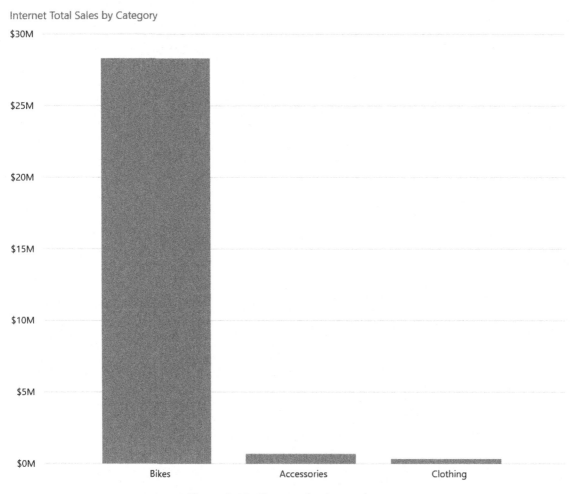

Internet Total Sales by Category

Figure 3.19: Clustered column chart

Power BI offers flexibility by providing different visualization options for the same dataset.

6. Click on the same diagram (**Internet Total Sales by Category**), and in the **Visualizations** tab, change it to a **Matrix**:

Figure 3.20: Selecting matrix format for visualization

Power BI will then create a table for total internet sales by categories.

Category	Internet Total Sales
Bikes	$28,318,144.65
Accessories	$700,759.96
Clothing	$339,772.61
Total	**$29,358,677.22**

Figure 3.21: Matrix visualization of Internet Total Sales by Category

Our next task is to understand the regions of the country with the most sales.

7. Navigate to the **Internet Sales** field and click on **Internet Total Sales** and then go to **Geography** field and select **Country Region Name**. Power BI will then create a clustered column chart. Change the Visualization to a **Donut chart** or **Pie chart** in order to quickly glance the performance correlations across regions. If you hover over a slice of a donut or pie, you will see some indicative metrics about that region:

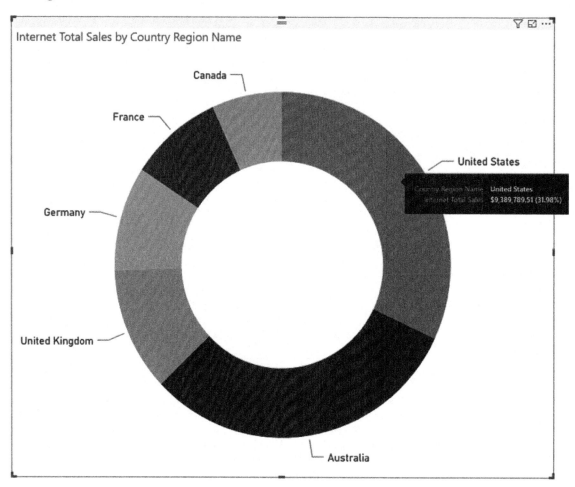

Figure 3.22: Internet Total Sales by Region Donut chart

8. Alongside the chart, use the same data field (**Country Region Name** and **Internet Total Sales**) and use a **Filled Map** visualization item instead. Power BI will show a map view of your worldwide sales. If you click on an item, all the other charts will react on the associated values from it.

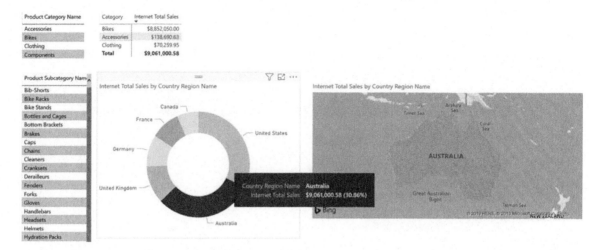

Figure 3.23: Filled map visualization of Total sales by region

9. Now add a graph of **Internet Total Sales by Year**. Click on **Internet Total Sales** in the **Internet Sales** field, and follow this up by clicking on **Fiscal** in the **Date** field. This will create a clustered column chart, as shown in the following diagram.

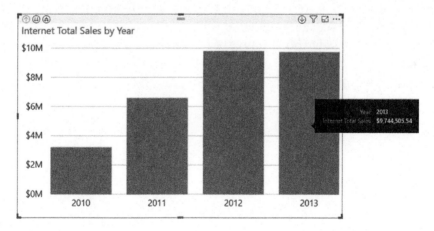

Figure 3.24: Total Internet Sales by Year: Clustered column chart

10. The last chart that we will create is just an association between the customers and internet sales. Click on the same **Internet Total Sales** field from **Internet Sales** and this time associate it with the **Commute Distance** and **Gender** fields from Customer. Change the visualization to a clustered bar chart.

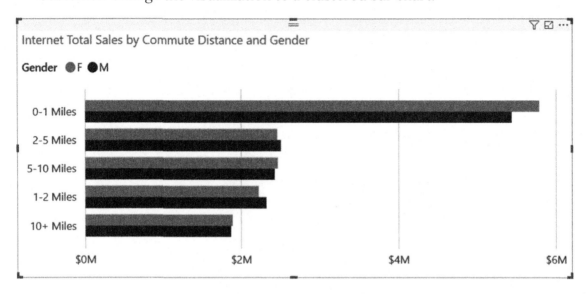

Figure 3.25: Total Sales by Commute Distance and Gender: Bar chart

This helps you to gain some insights about your customers. Most of those who buy your products are the ones within 1 mile commute from their work. This makes sense since `AdventureWorks` are selling bikes and related equipment. People who buy bikes are most likely those who are within cycling distance to work. You can also see that there is no major difference between genders in terms of your sales, and the indicative metric is the commute distance instead.

11. To add some styles to your dashboard, click on the **Switch Theme** ribbon near the top of the app. Feel free to choose the color of your choice.

Figure 3.26: Adding styles to your dashboard

You're now ready to save the dashboard to your workspace and share this graph with your colleagues.

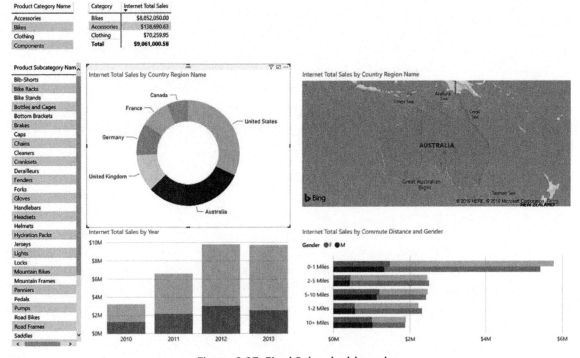

Figure 3.27: Final Sales dashboard

In this section, we saw the capabilities of Power BI in creating rich graphs with just a few clicks and drag-and-drops using Power BI Desktop. From semantic data models, we can represent meaningful data that can easily be understood by users.

Publishing the Dashboard

Now that you have created your graphs and dashboard, it is time to publish it to your workspace by performing the following steps:

1. Click on the **Publish** icon in the ribbon near the top of the app. Select a destination workspace. For this activity, feel free to select 'My workspace' as your destination.

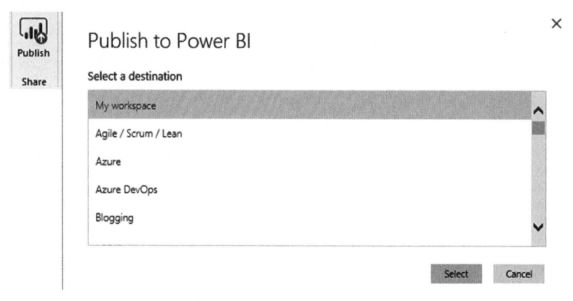

Figure 3.28: Publishing the dashboard to Power BI

Wait for Power BI to finish publishing the reports. Once published, it will show you a link where you can access the dashboard from a web page.

Figure 3.29: Publishing the dashboard to Power BI 2

2. You might need to log-in in order to access the dashboard.

Figure 3.30: Accessing the report from a webpage

3. On the top right-hand portion of the web page, click on **Share**.

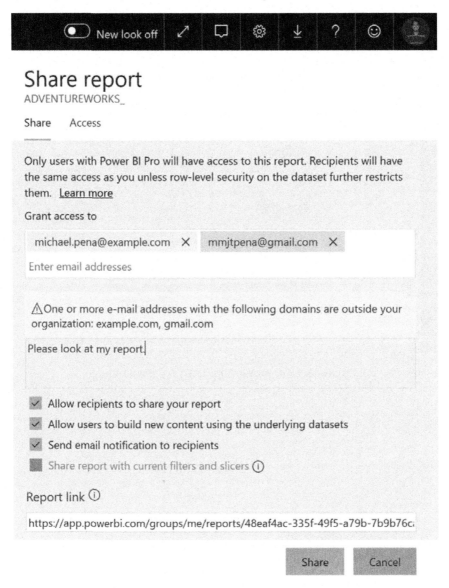

Figure 3.31: Sharing the report with multiple users

Feel free to share it with either your colleagues (in the same domain) or with guest users.

Users can also see a mobile version of the report by downloading the Power BI mobile app from the Apple iOS App Store or Google Play Store.

In the mobile app, you can see your own reports, as well as reports shared with your account. The following figure shows a mobile view of the **AdventureWorks** report we created earlier:

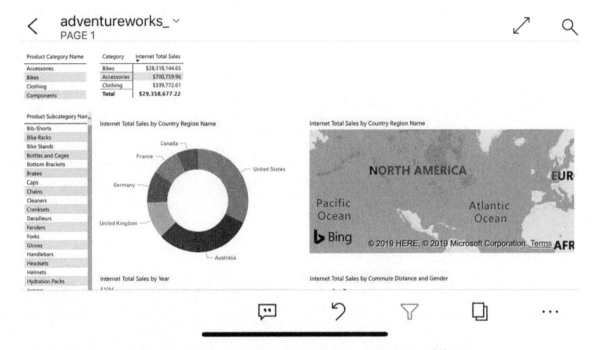

Figure 3.32: Accessing Power BI report on Power BI mobile app

You can then collaborate with your team and add comments and annotations to the report. This experience is very intuitive compared to sharing a PowerPoint presentation with your manager and colleagues.

In the next section, we will implement machine learning on Azure using Azure Machine Learning Services. We will also take a quick look at Azure Databricks in running a high-performance analysis of data sets.

Machine Learning on Azure

There are multiple ways to perform machine learning on Azure. Microsoft enables data science to be more accessible to all types of users and empowers data scientists to be more productive. Microsoft provides a suite of technologies for developers, database engineers and data scientists to create machine learning algorithms. Whatever your level of proficiency and expertise in Data Science, there is a useful Microsoft service, tool, or framework that can accelerate your machine learning journey.

The following figure depicts a machine learning landscape within the Microsoft Azure ecosystem. You can use pre-trained models using Azure cognitive services and directly integrate it with your applications without the need to set up a data pipeline. You can use popular frameworks like **TensorFlow** and **Keras** in Azure, whether installing it on a virtual machine or using a Machine Learning workspace. You can choose different platforms such as Azure Machine Learning services and Azure Databricks to prepare and run your ML experiments.

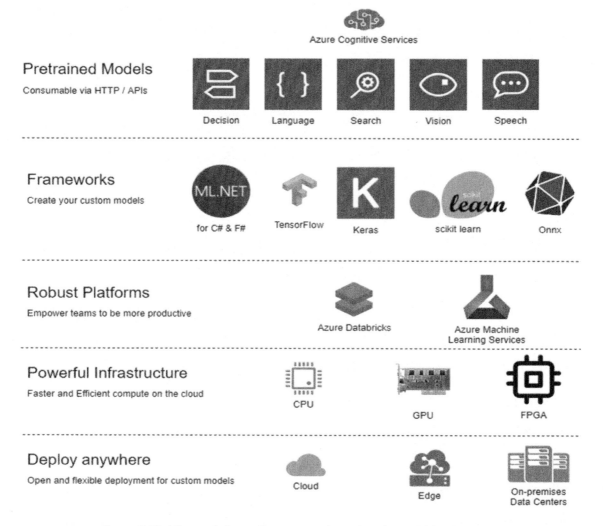

Figure 3.33: Microsoft Azure features and services for machine learning

By using Azure to drive your computation for machine learning analysis, you are provided with specialized hardware that can speed up your experiments. With accelerated hardware such as fast **graphics processing units** (**GPUs**) and **field-programmable gate arrays** (**FPGAs**), you can read billions of records and try various models concurrently to achieve faster results for your ML experiments.

The following sections will give an overview of the major technologies and platforms that implement machine learning and AI within the Microsoft Azure ecosystem.

ML.NET

ML.NET is an open-source cross-platform framework for **.NET** developers. By using ML.NET, you and your team can leverage existing skills, libraries, and frameworks that are already present within the .NET ecosystem. You can create web applications using ASP.NET, mobile applications using **Xamarin**, Desktop applications using WPF, and even IoT using Windows IoT. You can also extend the ML model creation by using TensorFlow and **ONNX**. ML.NET provides out-of-the-box support for algorithms that enable sentiment analysis, product recommendation, object detection, sales forecasting, and many more real-world business scenarios.

For tasks such as regression and classification, both training and consumption can be carried out using ML.NET. Other than this, it also supports core data types, extensible pipelines, data structures, tooling support, advanced performance mathematics, and so on.

ML.NET can be installed from nuget.org. Nuget.org is a public repository of downloadable .NET packages, libraries, and frameworks that you can easily add to your .NET project.

AutoML

Automated Machine Learning (**AutoML**) is a Microsoft Research project that aims to make machine learning easier for everyone. AutoML is designed to automatically detect the best ML models for you. As of writing, AutoML is capable of automatically selecting the right algorithm and helping tune hyperparameters for forecasting, classification, and regression. This is very useful if you do not have a data scientist in your team.

AutoML helps users (developers, analysts or even data scientists) to implement machine learning without a high barrier of entry relating to programming languages, libraries, frameworks, and data science concepts. It allows companies to innovate, thanks to faster time-to-market by means of an iterative process, and to leverage data science best practices when running experiments.

However, its scope is currently limited, and it can only perform certain algorithms and create a limited set of data models at this moment in time.

Azure Machine Learning Studio

Azure Machine Learning Studio is a visual drag-and-drop tool that allows users to intuitively perform their machine learning experiments with no coding. This involves connecting data sources, performing analysis, and serving the trained model as a web service using an API key. Azure Machine Learning Studio supports basic machine learning algorithms that involve classification, regression, and clustering.

Azure Databricks

We have already covered Azure Databricks in the previous chapter in detail. Azure Databricks enables you to perform machine learning with the use of Databricks Runtime for Machine Learning (Databricks Runtime ML) on your virtual nodes. Databricks Runtime ML includes popular libraries such as TensorFlow, **PyTorch**, Keras, and **XGBoost** to perform ML analysis at scale. Databricks also handles the installation of these frameworks for you. Azure Databricks also has the capability to use **Apache Spark MLlib** and perform hyperparameter tuning with **MLFlow**.

Cognitive Services

Microsoft Cognitive Services is a suite of cloud-based, general-purpose, pre-trained models and APIs that can be consumed and extended for further training for specific use-cases. If, for example, you want to create an object detection AI that understands what a banana is, you might need to feed in more data to help the AI understand that the image contains a banana. Consuming cognitive services is done via HTTP and is **platform-agnostic**, meaning you can use any programming language and operating system. There are five main categories of cognitive services: decision, vision, speech, search, and language. You can readily integrate AI and ML with your mobile, web, desktop, or even IoT applications using cognitive services.

The speech-to-text and speaker-recognition capabilities of the Speech Services API are good examples of cognitive services. These capabilities allow you to transform speech data to text, translate it to other languages, and recognize the identity of the speaker without setting up a Machine Learning workspace that involves millions of data sets and a series of ML model experiments.

Using cognitive services is the best approach for those who want to easily integrate AI and ML in their applications with minimum data science knowledge. Microsoft offers very flexible pricing options where you only pay for what you use, and most of the services have free tiers for you to explore.

You can learn more about cognitive services at https://packt.live/2rSxQyw.

Bot Framework

Microsoft Bot Framework enables applications to build intelligent bots (often used for chatbots) to automate workflows. The Bot Framework is closely associated with Microsoft Cognitive Services like **Language Understanding Intelligence Service (LUIS)** and **QnA Maker**. QnA maker is an NLP (Natural Language Processing) service that accelerates the creation of conversation-based AI such as chatbots. With the Bot framework, developers can easily create a conversational AI that learns through training from utterances and intents. This framework also allows developers to easily publish the bot to various channels such as Microsoft Teams, Cortana, and Slack.

The Bot Framework is now widely adopted by large corporations such as banks and retail conglomerates for their **first level support**. For example, the Bank of Beirut used Azure Bot Framework to create the Digi Bob chatbot that assists users in applying for loans and avail other banking services. To learn more, read about this use case at https://packt.live/34cxRvm.

Using the Bot Framework, developers can deploy intelligent enterprise-grade bots that can easily translate inquiries and messages (intents) from users and respond with meaningful actions. These actions can include querying a data source or orchestrating a command to a system. You can learn more about the Bot Framework at https://packt.live/3313jvn.

There are more machine learning tools and products within the Microsoft ecosystem, such as:

- SQL Server Machine Learning Services
- Microsoft Machine Learning Server
- Azure Data Science Virtual Machine
- Windows ML
- MMLSpark
- Azure Notebooks
- Azure Batch
- ML Services on HDInsight
- ML on Power BI
- Azure Machine Learning for VS Code
- Running your own ML frameworks to a Linux container or server image

This book would not be able to cover all of the technologies mentioned above, so we instead focus on Azure Machine Learning Services. For more information on the above services, visit https://packt.live/342WNFU.

Azure Machine Learning Services Features and Benefits

AMLS offers a variety of features and flexibility to users of various backgrounds and expertise. AMLS can integrate into your existing data pipeline to perform tasks such as leveraging data from Azure Data Lake or Azure Synapse Analytics, and serving the models directly to Power BI. You can also use Azure Databricks to further automate the hardware clusters where you are running your machine learning experiments.

AMLS provides an end-to-end workspace to run your machine learning operations. With AMLS, you can create experiments using AutoML, Visual Interface, or the **Software Development Kit** (**SDK**) in your ML notebook. You can also create a portable data model that can run in a container. This model can then be published to ACI (Azure Container Instances).

Software Development Kit (SDK)

Azure Machine Learning serves a Python SDK that fully supports mature frameworks such as **MXNet**, TensorFlow, PyTorch, and **Scikit-learn**. You can import the SDKs into your experiments using either Jupyter Notebooks, Azure Notebooks, or even Visual Studio Code.

Visual Interface

You can also use a visual interface (with minimum coding required) to create and run experiments. The experience is similar to Azure Machine Learning Studio where you use a lot of drag-and-drop tools as well as connecting entities. This is an intuitive way to connect data sources and create an ML model to train and serve.

AutoML

AutoML is a mechanism to suggest the best algorithm to use in your experiments. It is a baked-in feature of AMLS. You can automate away time-intensive tasks such as data cleaning and choosing the right algorithms for your model. With AutoML, you can rapidly iterate over many combinations of algorithms and hyperparameters to help you find the best model for your desired outcome.

Flexible Deployment Targets

Microsoft and Azure do not limit your model deployment options. Even if you are managing your workspace and performing your analysis on the cloud, you are not locked into just deploying the outcome of your experiments to Azure. You have the option to deploy it on-premises and edge environments by using containers.

Accelerated ML Operations (MLOps)

In a modern data warehouse, the combination of Azure Databricks and Azure Machine Learning Services can accelerate your machine learning operations. Azure MLS can provide you an end-to-end workspace where you can connect data from various sources with Azure Synapse Analytics, prepare and train data models, deploy them to consumers such as Power BI, and then monitor and retrain them to improve the accuracy.

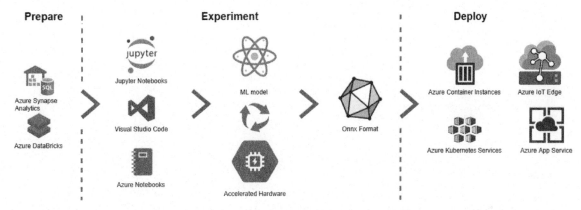

Figure 3.34: Preparation, Experiment, and Deployment in Azure Machine Learning Services

With Azure MLS you can use Azure Databricks to prepare the data for your experiments. You can then use either Jupyter notebooks or Visual Studio code to author your experiments; alternatively, you can also use the built-in Azure notebooks feature of MLS. You will then run your experiments to train and test your ML model by leveraging computers to run complex data science algorithms. It will then create an ML model with an ONNX format that is highly portable and can easily be deployed to a container such as Azure Container Instance. You also have the option to run it on AKS (Azure Kubernetes Services) or even on edge devices that support Docker.

This book will not cover the use of Azure Databricks as the compute cluster of Azure Machine Learning services. But there are advantages of having this combination. If you are already using Azure Databricks to derive real-time analytics on your modern data warehouse, you might also consider using it to run your ML experiments in Azure MLS.

You can read more about at https://packt.live/35ghoGG.

Quick Start Guide (Machine Learning)

Now that we have looked at what Microsoft can offer in the machine learning space, we will see a simple quick start guide on using Azure Machine Learning Services.

For this specific example, we will use the `Credit Card Fraud Detection` data set publicly available on Kaggle. Ideally in a modern data warehouse pipeline, you will get the data set from your warehouse.

Perform the following steps to build your ML model:

1. To start with, ensure your Azure portal is open, and then create a Machine Learning Service workspace on your Azure resource group. In the search bar, search for **Machine learning service workspace** and click on **Create**.

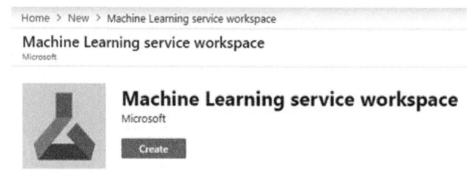

Figure 3.35: Creating a ML service workspace

2. Fill in the workspace name, subscription, resource group, and location. After reviewing, click on **Create**. Wait for the resource to be created. This may take several minutes.

3. Once a workspace is created, navigate here. Azure ML is a centralized general-purpose dashboard for your ML experiments.

4. Let us start by creating your first Compute cluster. Go to the **Compute** tab.

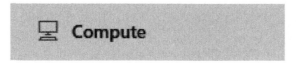

Figure 3.36: The Compute tab

5. Click on the **+ Add** button. Fill in the computer name. Choose **Machine Learning Compute** as your **Compute type**. The **Region** is pre-set from the workspace region. Choose a size for your machine; you can use a **Standard_DS12_v2** for starters. Choose **Dedicated** VM. Set **1** as the **Minimum number of nodes** and **6** as the **Maximum number of nodes**:

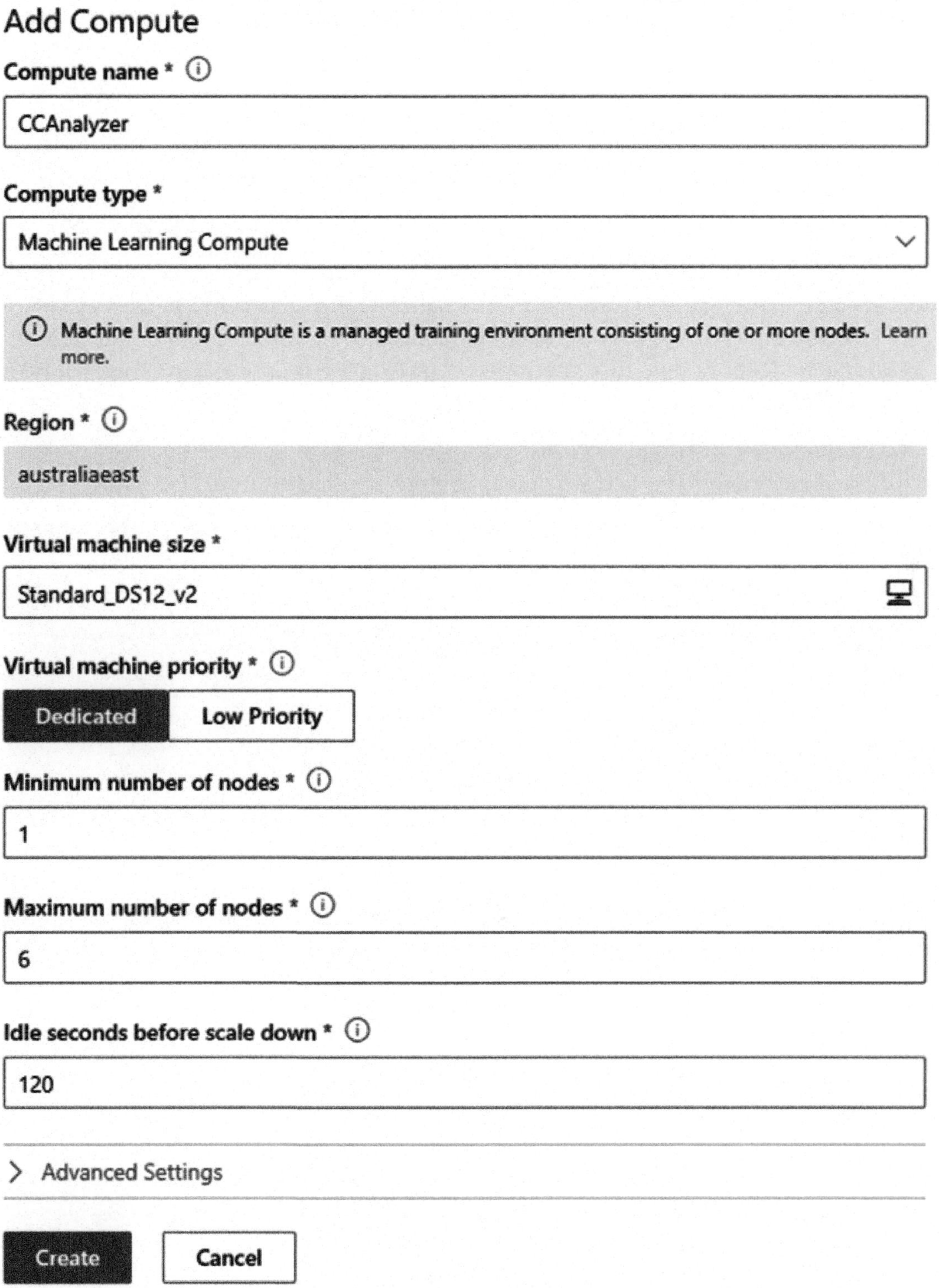

Add Compute

Compute name * ⓘ

CCAnalyzer

Compute type *

Machine Learning Compute ⌄

> ⓘ Machine Learning Compute is a managed training environment consisting of one or more nodes. Learn more.

Region * ⓘ

australiaeast

Virtual machine size *

Standard_DS12_v2 🖥

Virtual machine priority * ⓘ

| Dedicated | Low Priority |

Minimum number of nodes * ⓘ

1

Maximum number of nodes * ⓘ

6

Idle seconds before scale down * ⓘ

120

> Advanced Settings

Create   Cancel

Figure 3.37: Adding compute details

6. Click on **Create**. Wait for the cluster to be provisioned. Once the provision state has changed to **Succeeded**, then you can now use the nodes of it to run your experiments.

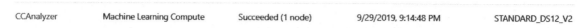

CCAnalyzer   Machine Learning Compute   Succeeded (1 node)   9/29/2019, 9:14:48 PM   STANDARD_DS12_V2

Figure 3.38: Provisioned state of machine learning compute

7. Visit kaggle (https://packt.live/35lfEMF) and download the **csv** file (click on Download and unzip the folder).

8. Go back to Azure ML and click on Datasets tab at the navigation pane. Click on **+ Create dataset** and choose **From local files**. Upload the **csv** file that you downloaded from Kaggle. Use a creative name for your dataset and then set the type as **Tabular**.

   In the **Advanced settings**, you will see that it will upload the file to the ML workspace storage. Optionally, you can change the location for the datastore.

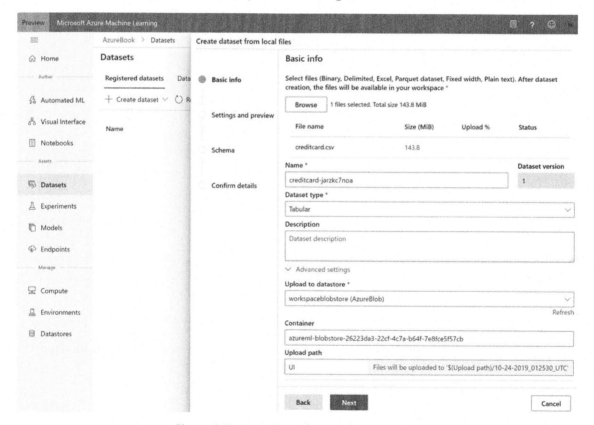

Figure 3.39: Creating a dataset from csv file

9. Click on done. Wait for it to upload the file.

10. Now go to the **Automated ML** tab on the left-hand side navigation. Create a new experiment by clicking on **+ Create experiment**.

11. Set the experiment name. Select a training compute by choosing the compute cluster that you created earlier in *step* 5. For the dataset, choose the `csv` file that you uploaded to the datastore (the `creditcard csv` from Kaggle).

    AML will then show a preview of the data set. A lot of the data fields are anonymized for security purposes. This involves PCA dimensionality reduction.

Figure 3.40: dataset preview as displayed by AML

12. In the prediction task, choose **Classification** to classify transactions as either fraudulent or non-fraudulent.

13. For the `target column`, choose `Class`, as this is the outcome of whether the transaction is fraudulent or not.

14. In the advanced settings, add the following values:

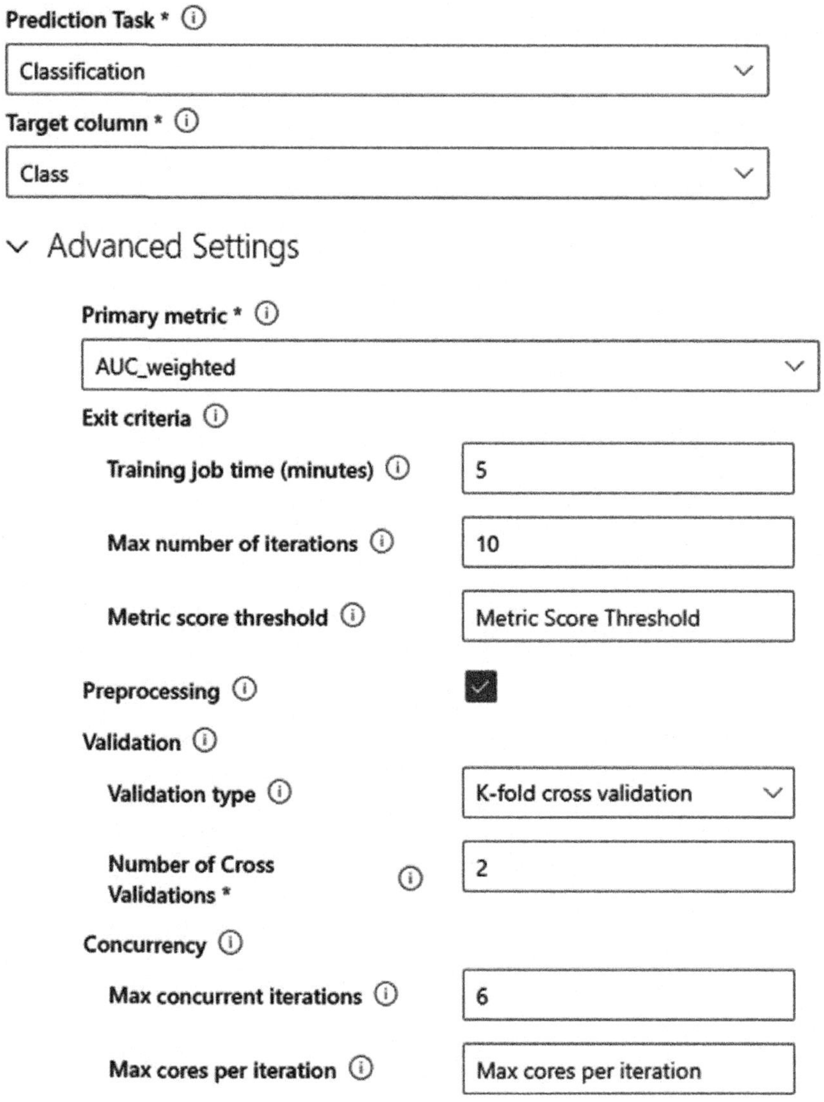

Prediction Task * ⓘ

```
Classification                                                    ⌄
```

Target column * ⓘ

```
Class                                                             ⌄
```

⌄ Advanced Settings

Primary metric * ⓘ

```
AUC_weighted                                                      ⌄
```

Exit criteria ⓘ

Training job time (minutes) ⓘ	5
Max number of iterations ⓘ	10
Metric score threshold ⓘ	Metric Score Threshold

Preprocessing ⓘ ☑

Validation ⓘ

Validation type ⓘ	K-fold cross validation ⌄
Number of Cross Validations * ⓘ	2

Concurrency ⓘ

Max concurrent iterations ⓘ	6
Max cores per iteration ⓘ	Max cores per iteration

Figure 3.41: Adding details to the classification algorithm

Note

AUC_weighted is the arithmetic mean of the score for each class, weighted by the number of true instances in each class.

K-fold cross-validation is a resampling procedure that splits that dataset into K groups to evaluate machine learning models on a limited data sample.

Note that you can increase the values of the parameters above if you want to either run more concurrent tests or increase the training times. This will affect your compute consumption and running times. You can also set some options to block algorithms if they don't fit your scenario.

15. Click on **Start**.

Azure MLS will then run and try different algorithms to achieve the desired outcome. Based on your configuration in the previous steps, it can run concurrent and simultaneous algorithms to train your model. Running this will take some time.

Once this is completed, you will see the formula that achieved the highest score. This method will allow you to test out different formulae to understand if a transaction is fraudulent or not.

You can deploy this model to an **Azure Container Instance** (**ACI**) and then later deploy to other container-supported devices such as IoT devices.

These scores can never be 100% accurate, but once we have developed a model we can filter new transactions and detect whether they may be fraudulent.

The following figure shows that by using **VotingEnsemble**, you can achieve 98% accuracy in predicting whether an incoming transaction is fraudulent.

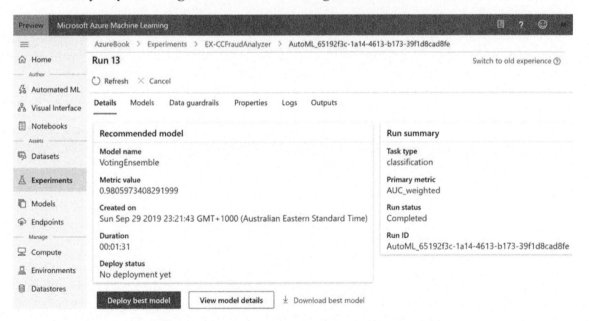

Figure 3.42: Credit card fraud model iteration chart

This exercise can get you started with Machine Learning on Azure. You were able to run ML algorithms and classify a complex data set within minutes without coding. You can further refine your experiments by increasing the number of iterations, or by increasing the training time.

If you want to learn more about the meaning of the graphs, you can refer to https://packt.live/2Qwb7CJ.

After these exercises, feel free to delete the resources from the Azure portal to ensure that your workspaces will not continuously bill your subscription.

Summary

In this chapter, we discussed semantic modeling with Azure Analysis Services. Using AAS, we created a bridge between the data source and data visualization. We then explored Power BI Desktop to create reports. Power BI enables you to create rich and meaningful graphs that derive business insights. We then published the report in order to collaborate on it across different media.

We have learned that there are many available tools and technologies to implement ML and AI in Azure. We have explored Machine Learning Services, its features and benefits, and performed Machine Learning on Azure to predict credit card fraud detection. In the next chapter, we will discuss the new features and functionalities added to the modern data warehouse.

Introducing Azure Synapse Analytics

In previous chapters, you learned about the modern data warehouse patterns and how to implement your own end-to-end modern data warehouse using Azure services. This chapter presents a high-level preview of Azure Synapse Analytics, an exciting new suite of functionalities being added to the Microsoft data warehouse.

What is Azure Synapse Analytics?

Azure Synapse is a limitless analytics service that brings together enterprise data warehousing and big data analytics. It gives you the freedom to do data queries in a way that suits the needs of your business. You can utilize serverless on-demand or provisioned resources, and this can be done, at scale. Azure Synapse brings these together with a unified experience to ingest, prepare, manage, and serve data for immediate business intelligence and machine learning needs.

Azure Synapse is the next evolution of Azure SQL Data Warehouse. Microsoft has taken the industry leading data warehouses to a new level of performance and capabilities (https://packt.live/2QwXKSF). Businesses can continue running their existing data warehouse workloads in production with Azure Synapse and will automatically benefit from the new capabilities which are in preview. Businesses can put their data to work much more quickly, productively, and securely, pulling together insights from all data sources, data warehouses, and big data analytics systems.

With Azure Synapse, data professionals of all types can collaborate, manage, and analyze their most important data with ease—all within the same service. From Apache Spark integration with the powerful and trusted SQL engine, to code-free data integration and management, Azure Synapse is built for every data professional.

At the time of this publication, the enterprise data warehousing features in Azure Synapse are generally available, and new features (such as on-demand query and Apache Spark integration) are in private preview. Features described in this chapter are subject to change.

The following figure gives an overview of the new services and features available in Azure Synapse Analytics:

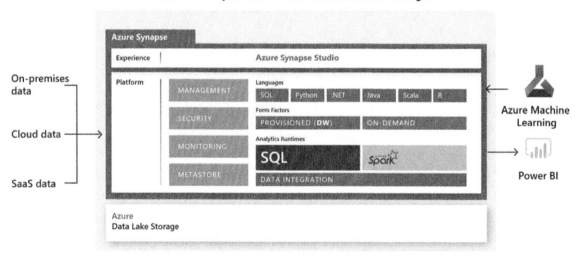

Figure 4.1: Azure Synapse Analytics

Why do we need Azure Synapse Analytics?

One challenge that businesses face today is the need to manage two types of analytics systems:

- **Data warehouse,** which provides critical insights about the business
- **Data lakes,** which provide meaningful insights about customers, products, employees, and processes through various analytics methodologies

Both of these analytics systems are critical to businesses and operate independently of one another. This can lead to uninformed decisions. At the same time, businesses need to unlock insights from all their data to stay competitive and to innovate processes to obtain better results.

For customers wanting to build their own end-to-end data pipeline, they must go through the following steps:

1. Ingest data from various data sources
2. Load all these data sources into a data lake for further processing
3. Data cleaning over a range of different data structures and types
4. Prepare, transform, and model the data
5. Serve the cleansed data to thousands of users through BI tools and applications

Until now, each of these steps has required a different tool, and with so many different tools, services, and applications on offer, choosing the right one can be daunting.

There are numerous services that ingest, load, prepare and serve data. There are also multiple services based on the developer's language of choice to use for data cleaning. Some developers prefer to use Spark, and some want to use SQL, while others want code-free environments to transform the data.

Even once the right collection of tools have been chosen, there is a steep learning curve to get to grip with them, plus the logistical difficulties of maintaining a data pipeline over different platforms and languages. With such a range of issues, implementing and maintaining a cloud analytics platform can be a difficult task.

The Modern Data Warehouse Pattern

As demonstrated in *Chapter 2, Building Your Modern Data Warehouse*, Azure offers one of the best and easiest-to-understand modern data warehouse patterns with the following services:

- **Azure Data Factory**, which helps you ingest data from data sources to the **Azure Data Lake Storage** and orchestrate the data pipeline.

- **Azure Databricks** and **HDInsight,** which provide you with Spark capabilities, so you can use Python, Scala, .NET, Java, R, to prepare and analyze the data as well as build machine learning models to process the data.

- **Azure Synapse Analytics,** which is primarily used for analytics purposes.

- Additional services that are highly optimized to serve concurrent queries up to **Power BI** dashboards or applications for visualization.

This modern data warehouse pattern seamlessly brings all these services together to create the end-to-end pipeline.

Customer Challenges

You might think that the biggest challenge for an efficient data warehouse is learning how to build the pipeline to bring the data in or optimizing the warehouse to get better performance. However, in a customer study conducted by Microsoft, it was concluded that the biggest customer challenge was managing different capabilities, monitoring hundreds of pipelines spanning across various compute engines, securing different resources (compute, storage, artifacts), and deploying code without breaking changes. Between organizational silos, data silos, and tooling silos, it becomes nearly impossible to implement and maintain a cloud analytics platform.

For example, imagine your company needed to come up with a single security model to protect all of its services to meet the latest internal compliance guidelines. A task like this might at first sound straightforward, but in fact, it is quite involved. You need to quickly identify what that "single security model" is, and then have to figure out what the deployment model is across these services. You need to work out how to implement high availability and disaster recovery for each of these services. And finally, you need to look after all the related lifecycle management responsibilities, including monitoring these services to ensure that are performing well. Bringing all these services together is no small endeavor, and in the past has required complex planning.

Azure Synapse Analytics Comes to the Rescue

Azure Synapse Analytics solves these problems. It simplifies the entire modern data warehouse pattern, allowing customers to build end-to-end analytics solutions with a unified experience.

The Azure Synapse studio provides a unified UI for data prep, data management, data warehousing, big data analytics, and AI tasks. It offers the following features:

- Code-free visual environments for managing data pipelines

- Automated query optimization

- The functionality to build proofs of concept in minutes

- Serverless on-demand queries

- The option to securely access datasets and use Power BI to build dashboards in minutes—all while using the same analytics service

Azure Synapse Analytics can derive and deliver insights from all your data lying in the data warehouse and big data analytics systems at lightning-fast speeds. It enables data professionals to use familiar SQL language to query both relational and non-relational databases at petabyte-scale. Advanced features like intelligent workload management, workload isolation, and limitless concurrency help optimize the performance of all queries for mission-critical workloads.

Azure Synapse Analytics is taking the best of the Azure SQL Data Warehouse, modernizing it by providing more functionalities for the SQL developers, adding serverless on-demand query, adding machine learning support, embedding Spark natively, providing collaborative Notebooks, and offering data integration within a single service. It supports different languages (such as C#, SQL, Scala, Python), all through different engines. In the following diagram you can see the Azure Synapse Analytics architecture.

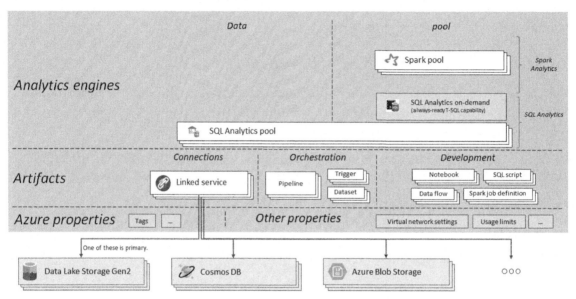

Figure 4.2: Azure Synapse Analytics architecture

By using Azure Synapse Analytics, customers can carry out business intelligence projects and machine learning with ease. Azure Synapse Analytics is deeply integrated with Power BI and Azure Machine Learning to greatly expand the discovery of insights from all your data and apply machine learning models to all your intelligent apps. The user can significantly reduce project development time for BI and machine learning projects with a limitless analytics service that enables you to seamlessly apply intelligence over all your most important data—from Dynamics 365 and Office 365 to Software as a Service (SaaS) implementations that support Open Data Initiative (https://packt.live/2CWxb1p)—and easily share data (https://packt.live/2CZR0EQ) with just a few clicks.

This is all provided in a single experience which features query editors and notebooks for sharing and collaborating data, as well as assets and code for both SQL and Spark developers.

Essentially, Azure Synapse Analytics does it all.

Deep Dive into Azure Synapse Analytics

Now that you know why Azure Synapse Analytics was invented, you can take a deeper look at Azure Synapse Analytics services.

Azure Synapse Analytics is a fully-managed, integrated data analytics service that blends data warehousing, data integration, and big data processing with accelerating time to insight into a single service.

The advantage of having a single integrated data service is that, for enterprises, it accelerates the delivery of business intelligence, artificial intelligence, machine learning, Internet of Things, and intelligent applications. The following figure shows the single integrated data service offered by Azure:

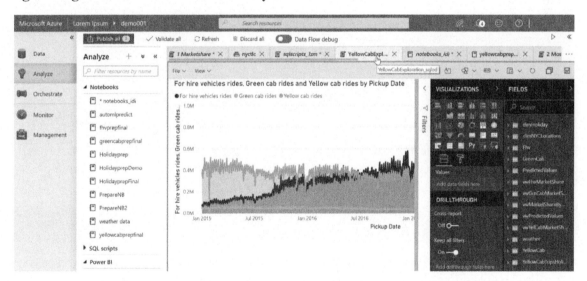

Figure 4.3: Analyzing and Visualizing data in Azure Synapse Analytics

To fully appreciate the benefits of Azure Synapse, you should first take a look at its core services.

Azure Synapse Analytics Workspaces

At the heart of Azure Synapse, is the workspace. A workspace is the top-level resource which comprises your analytics solution in the data warehouse. The Azure Synapse workspace supports both relational and big data processing. Its collaborative environment is an ideal place for data engineers and data scientists to share and collaborate their analytics solutions, as shown in the following figure:

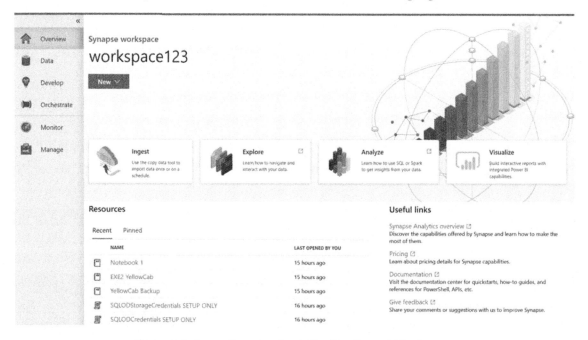

Figure 4.4: Azure Synapse Analytics Studio and Workspace

Key Features

Azure Synapse Analytics workspace provides the following features:

- A fast, highly elastic, secure data warehouse

- Ability to run concurrent T-SQL queries through SQL Pools across petabytes of data to serve BI tools and applications

- SQL On-Demand provides serverless SQL queries for ease of exploration and analysis of data in Azure Data Lake Storage without any setup or maintenance of infrastructure

- Meets the full range of analytics needs, from data engineering to data science, using a variety of languages, such as Python, Scala, C#, and Spark SQL

- Spark pools, which alleviate the complex setup and maintenance of clusters and simplify the development of Spark applications and usage of Spark Notebooks

- Offers deep integration between Spark and SQL, allowing Data Engineers to prepare data in Spark, write the processed results in SQL Pool, and use any combination of Spark with SQL for data engineering and analysis, with built-in support for Azure Machine Learning

- Highly scalable, hybrid data integration capability that accelerates data ingestion and operationalization through automated data pipelines

- Provides a friction-free integrated service with unified security, deployment, monitoring, and billing

Azure Synapse Analytics Studio

The Azure Synapse studio features a user-friendly, web-based interface that provides an end-to-end workspace and development experience.

The following figure shows an example of a modern data pipeline using Azure Synapse. In this example, the ingestion starts from a Blob storage source into an Azure Data Lake Storage in the Azure Synapse Analytics Workspace. Using the Spark Pool, you can read multiple data sources from the Azure Data Lake and SQL Database and perform any transformation and data cleansing. Finally, you can write the curated results in the SQL Pool to serve BI tools and applications.

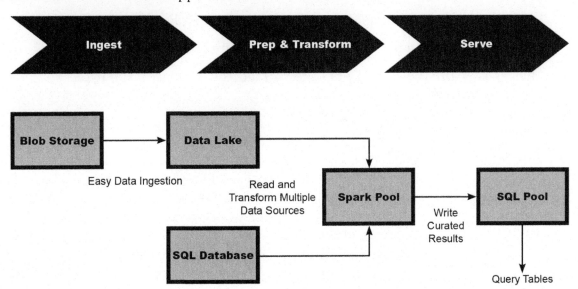

Figure 4.5: Modern Data Pipeline using Azure Synapse Analytics

The following sections will highlight the capabilities, key features, platform details and end-user services:

Capabilities

- A fast, highly elastic, secure data warehouse with industry leading performance and security

- Ability to explore Azure Data Lake Storage and data warehouse using familiar T-SQL syntax in SQL On-demand (serverless) SQL queries

- Apache Spark integrated with Azure Machine Learning

- Hybrid data integration to accelerate data ingestion and operationalization of analytics process (ingest, prepare, transform, and serve)

- Business report generation and serving with Power BI integration

Key Features

- Directly explore data in your Azure Data Lake Storage, data warehouse, as well as any external connections to the workspace, using Azure Synapse Analytics Studio

- Create and operationalize pipelines for data ingestion and orchestration

- Write code using Notebooks and T-SQL query editors

- Code-free data transformation tool, if you prefer not to write your own code

- Monitor, secure, and manage your workspaces without leaving the environment

- Web-based development experience for the entire analytics solutions

- Ability to explore the Azure Data Lake Storage, the databases, and external connections to the workspace

Platform

- Supports both provisioned and serverless computes. Examples of provisioned computes include SQL Computes and Spark Computes. These provisioned computes allow teams to segment their compute resources so that they can control cost and usage to better align with their organizational structure. Serverless computes, on the other hand, allow teams to use the service on demand without provisioning or managing any underlying infrastructure.

- Deep integration between Spark and SQL engines

New Preview Features

At the time of this publication, the following features are available in private preview.

To nominate yourself for access to private preview features, please apply at https://packt.live/2puhcEA.

Apache Spark

For customers who want Apache Spark, it has first-party support through Azure Databricks and is fully managed by Azure. The latest version of Apache Spark will automatically be made available to users, along with all security patches.

If you use Spark within Azure Synapse Analytics, it is provided as a SaaS. For example, you can use Spark without setting up or managing your own services, such as a virtual network. Azure Synapse Analytics will take care of the underlying infrastructure for you. This allows you to use Spark immediately in your Azure Synapse Analytics environment.

SQL On-Demand

SQL On-Demand provides serverless SQL queries. This allows ease of exploration and data analysis in Azure Data Lake Storage without any setup or infrastructure maintenance:

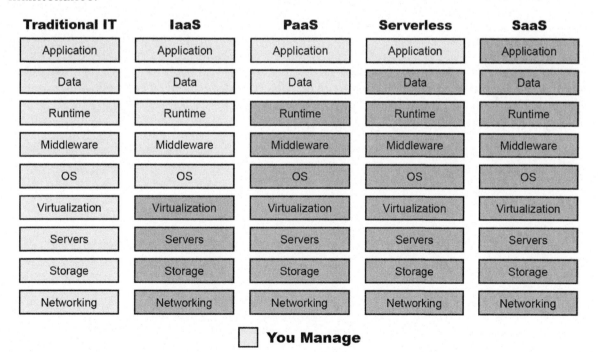

Figure 4.6: Comparison between different infrastructures

Key Features

- Analysts can focus on analyzing the data without worrying about managing any infrastructure.

- Customers can benefit from the simple and flexible pricing model, as they only pay for what they use.

- It uses the familiar T-SQL language syntax and the best SQL Query Optimizer on the market. The SQL Query Optimizer is the brain behind the query engine.

- You can easily scale your compute and storage, independent of one another, as your needs grow.

- Seamlessly integrate with SQL Analytics Pool and Spark via metadata sync and native connectors.

For example, you can query your Azure Data Lake Storage using familiar T-SQL syntax by following these steps:

1. Select a file from your Azure Data Lake Storage.

2. Right-click and run your SQL On-Demand (serverless) SQL query using T-SQL syntax (for example, GROUP BY, ORDER BY, etc.).

Data Integration

Azure Synapse Analytics uses the Azure Data Factory (ADF) technology to provide data integration features. The key features of the ADF that are essential to the modern data warehouse pipeline are available in Azure Synapse Analytics. All these features are wrapped with a common security model, role-based access control (RBAC) in the Azure Synapse Analytics Workspace.

The following figure shows an example of the data pipeline and the activities from ADF that are directly integrated inside the Azure Synapse Analytics environment:

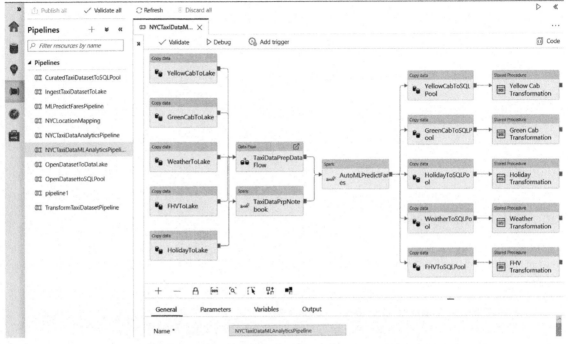

Figure 4.7: Data Pipelines in Azure Synapse Analytics

Key Features

- Integrated platform services for management, security, monitoring, and metadata management

- Native integration between Spark and SQL. Single line of code to read and write with Spark from/into SQL analytics

- Ability to create a Spark table and query it instantaneously with SQL Analytics without defining schema

- Common Data Model aware

- "Key free" environment. With Single Sign-On and AAD pass-through, no key or login is needed to interact with ADLS/Databases

Multiple language support

Azure Synapse Analytics supports multiple languages suited to different analytics workloads:

- SQL
- Python
- C#
- Java
- Scala
- R

Upcoming Changes

As a product evolves, it is sometimes necessary to realign a product by updating its name. The following table indicates the name changes/updates that will be applicable henceforth.

Service / Capability / Resources	Before	After
Service	Azure SQL Data Warehouse	Azure Synapse Analytics
Capability		SQL Analytics Pool
Compute Resource	SQL Data Warehouse	SQL Pool
Storage Resource		Database

Figure 4.8: Upcoming changes

Summary

Azure Synapse Analytics is a groundbreaking evolution of Azure SQL Data Warehouse. It enables data professionals to build end-to-end analytics solutions with a unified experience.

Azure Synapse takes the best of the Azure SQL Data Warehouse, modernizing it by providing more functionalities for the SQL developers, adding serverless on-demand query, adding machine learning support, embedding Spark natively, providing collaborative Notebooks, and offering data integration—all within a single service.

The existing Azure services described in the modern data warehouse pattern (which you learned in the previous chapters) will continue to thrive. With its new features, Microsoft will offer a simplified and streamlined approach for customers to build their analytics solutions.

You can try these preview features today. To nominate yourself for access to private preview features, please apply at https://packt.live/2puhcEA.

In the next chapter, you will see real use cases on how all of these technologies are integrated to provide the complete end-to-end data warehouse solutions business decision-makers can use to derive meaningful insights from real-time data.

5

Business Use Cases

In the previous chapters, you learned about cloud-scale analytics and the services Microsoft Azure offers to empower businesses to discover insights. You were also introduced to the new features and functionalities added to the modern data warehouse. In this chapter, you will look at two real-world business use cases to demonstrate high-level solutions using Microsoft Azure. The aim of these use cases is to illustrate how real-time data can be analyzed in Azure to derive meaningful insights and make business decisions.

The company names used here are fictitious, and for the implementation demos, we use sample datasets. However, the business use cases, the challenges, and the actual problems are real. They illustrate the kinds of data problems you might encounter in your everyday life.

The first business case focuses on helping a company gain actionable insights from its data in near real time. The second one talks about using Data Analytics on Azure to address operational issues and offer better services to passengers by improving the utilization of the infrastructure of Egypt's busiest airport. For each of the use cases, we will first briefly discuss the problem and the challenges, and then look at a potential solution design and the Azure services that enables such solutions.

Use Case 1: Real-Time Customer Insights with Azure Synapse Analytics

Contoso is a large multinational retail company that has stores in Australia, New Zealand, and Japan. The company sells consumer goods, electronics, and personal care items through its brick-and-mortar stores and digital online channels (mobile and web applications).

Contoso has appointed a new chief executive officer who is passionate about data, and she has set up a new data analytics team and tasked it with creating and maintaining customer insights in near real-time to drive business decisions.

The Problem

Contoso, like many other organizations, is trying to reinvent itself as a data-driven company. There are many indicators that show that this is the right strategy. However, for Contoso to succeed, it has to solve many problems. Some of these problems are technical, while others are cultural and organizational.

Contoso's CEO wants the new data analytics team to help the business answer questions that guide operational decisions. There are many questions that the executive team is hoping to answer with data. However, to better articulate the scope of this project, the Contoso data team (in consultation with the CEO) agreed to define the problem statement as follows:

How can Contoso increase profits?

More specifically, the Contoso data team is given a 20-day challenge to run a pilot data analytics program to model ways to help Contoso increase its profit margin by 10%.

The team will start by focusing on two key areas:

- Understanding customers' purchasing behaviors to predict product sales. This includes optimizing logistics operations, use of shelf space, and reducing the waste of expired products.

- Using customer, sales, and marketing data to optimize Contoso's spending on promotions and marketing to reach the right customers with the right promotion.

Excited to accomplish this task, the Contoso data team started with a workshop to refine the requirements and technical challenges. Contoso's current data practices, like most companies, are geared towards reporting what happened in the past. Current reports answer questions such as "How many products were sold?" and "What was the revenue generated by product A?". However, this is very different from what Contoso is trying to achieve, which is to discover patterns to predict what products Contoso should sell and in what quantities they will sell them, and doing so in near real-time. For this to happen, the Contoso data team concluded that they need to tackle the following challenges.

Capturing and Processing New Data

Contoso interacts with its customers via multiple physical and digital channels. Each of these interactions generates data that can be valuable to Contoso. Think of all the transactions at the store checkout, customer responses to varying advertisements, and aisle adjustments on the store floor, as well as any loyalty card points that they might have earned. Each customer interaction generates a variety of data that Contoso needs to capture.

Furthermore, Contoso's online store has trackers and beacons to record customers' activities and their responses to products that are on promotion. Contoso's mobile application has similar functionality that enables Contoso to create a very good view of what customers like and dislike. Contoso uses a mix of Azure Application Insights and Splunk, as well as internal tools for recording users' click events, navigations, time spent on each page, what products are added to the shopping cart, and how many orders are finalized. Combining this data with application logs, network monitoring events, and what Contoso already knows about its customers provides a powerful tool for Contoso to predict usage trends and patterns.

Contoso not only needs to capture and store all this data from physical and digital customer interactions, but it also needs to clean, validate, prepare, and aggregate all this data. This is a massive task that the team has not had experience with before. The team used to batch process data by loading historical data into the data warehouse to generate daily and weekly reports. This is quite challenging for the team, being an exciting but also mammoth task.

Bringing All the Data Together

Usually, data comes in various formats and shapes. For instance, purchase transactions are highly structured tabular data that is easy to work with. Application logs, on the other hand, are semi-structured files that list millions of events and trace messages of what happens on the application's servers. Contoso needs to ingest both of these types of data: structured and unstructured data.

To make things even more interesting, social media feeds are unstructured and are in a natural language that customers use to write on the web. These feeds can be very valuable to Contoso, as they inform the company of the actual feedback provided by their customer base. However, for data practitioners, it's hard to capture and organize these loose feeds of natural language posts in the same format and shape as the highly structured transaction data.

The data team at Contoso needs to face the challenges of not only capturing data in all of its varying forms (structured, semi-structured, and unstructured), but also find a way to clean and store all this data in one place so that it can be joined and correlated with other forms of data from other sources to discover new insights.

Finding insights and Patterns in Data

Once all the data is captured, cleaned, validated, and stored, the Contoso data team needs to start the challenging task of finding meaningful insights and patterns in the data. However, this can be a complicated problem to solve. When we are talking about gigabytes (or potentially terabytes) of varying datasets, how do you find these patterns? Where do you start?

Traditional reporting and statistical techniques will not scale and can't be used alone to tackle this challenge. Conventional forms of programming are not very useful as the programmers and the data practitioners themselves do not know what they are looking for or how to find these insights.

Real-time Discovery

Contoso needs to discover meaningful insights quickly and action any findings as soon as such insights are discovered. Data usually loses its value with time, and some data loses its value directly after ingestion. For instance, imagine a scenario where Contoso is running a major promotion on a particular product, say ABC-brand soft drink. This drink is selling very fast today in stores X, Y, and Z. It would have no great value if Contoso discovered this trend tomorrow because, by that time, stores X, Y, and Z will have empty shelves and customers will be disappointed that they did not get their desired product, meaning Contoso will have lost good opportunities to sell more.

As a result, Contoso is aiming to discover insights and trends in real-time or near real-time. Contoso defines near real-time as being 5-10 seconds behind real-time. This gives just enough time for data pipelines to process and analyze live data as it is generated in Contoso.

Contoso's CEO has made it clear to the team that the organization needs to know in near real-time how its operations are running and how the customers feel about its brand and services. She mentioned a scenario where Contoso had just decided to discontinue selling product A. After this decision, customers started having many discussions on social media platforms. Then Contoso's CEO posed the following question: What if a large number of Contoso's customers were talking online about potentially switching to a competitor of Contoso just because of that decision? The answer to that question is a piece of information that is critical to Contoso and could be detrimental to its success. The CEO's point is that having the ability to analyze, find, and act on insights in real time can be a massive competitive advantage for Contoso.

To summarize, Contoso is facing the following challenges:

- Contoso wants to capture and store large datasets from varying data sources with potentially high throughput. These data sources include transactional data stores, **Internet of Things** (**IoT**) sensors, Contoso's online stores, and application log files.

- The company also wants to combine structured, semi-structured, and unstructured data to create one single dataset through joining and correlating data from multiple sources.

- Contoso needs to handle the varying granularity and quality levels of the different data points. The team needs to clean, prepare, transform, and join these multiple datasets.

- Contoso wants to draw meaningful insights and patterns from the data in near real-time.

- Finally, the company wants to scale this data discovery process to meet the demands of the business.

Design Brainstorming

The following few sections will try to better articulate the requirements and come up with a technical solution that could satisfy these requirements.

Data Ingestion

The first task for any data practitioner is to look for data, collect it, clean it, validate it, and then start the exciting part of data discovery and exploration. For the current scenario, you need to define the data sources you need to pull data from. You also need to look at how you can load data from different sources to create one single dataset that can be explored and queried easily by data analysts. Some of the source systems that you need for this use case include:

- **Sales transactions**: The sales transactions can not only tell what and how many products were sold at a particular store, but they can also indicate what customers bought what products. This is because Contoso already has a loyalty program where customers scan their loyalty card as part of the checkout procedure. Contoso has two different data stores for sales transactions: one data store for physical stores and another one for Contoso's online stores.

- **Customer data**: Contoso has a **Customer Relationship Manager** (**CRM**) system that holds customer data. Customer data includes (among other things) first names, last names, home addresses, phone numbers, email addresses, and age group information.

- **Loyalty program data**: The loyalty program data is stored in a different source system, and it helps Contoso in linking customer data with sales transactions.

- **Digital applications clickstreams and usage data**: This indicates how Contoso's customers are responding to the design and content of Contoso's applications.

- **Sensors and IoT data**: Some of Contoso's stores are equipped with digital sensors to understand customer behaviors on the store floor. Some stores have IoT sensors installed to count how many customers walk past each aisle and at what time. There are also sensors to measure temperature and humidity in Contoso's stores. Contoso uses these sensors to ensure that fresh products such as milk are kept in the right conditions. Moreover, Contoso also has sensors for counting customer headcounts in near real time. This helps Contoso to deploy more staff during peak hours/rush hours to ensure faster service so the customers do not have to wait in long queues.

- **Other datasets**: To enrich Contoso's data and give it another dimension, the Contoso data team is considering pulling other data, such as weather data, **Geographical Information Systems** (**GIS**)/map data, suburb and city profile data, and other similar data from public datasets. These datasets can enrich Contoso's data and add greater context to the trends and patterns in customer behaviors and sales figures. Take the weather, for instance. Contoso might find that the sales of certain products might correlate with certain weather conditions—for example, increase in the sale of ice cream during the summer season. Similarly, a city profile with certain age group and average income attributes may have a strong correlation with the sales figures of certain products. For instance, suburbs where the average age is 25 might have higher sales of hair-styling products, while stores in suburbs with an average age of 45 might sell far less of the same products.

Data Storage

As explained previously, Contoso needs to ingest data from a variety of sources. Contoso also estimates the size of its current datasets to be over 400 TB with an average growth of 10-15 GB per day. The format of these datasets is also quite different. Some of them are highly structured, while others are fully unstructured. One common thing between all these different datasets is that they are all growing rapidly, and they arrive at a high throughput rate. To serve Contoso's needs, we need to have a data store that:

1. Is scalable and elastic to grow with the demands of Contoso's data team.

2. Is a secure and controlled platform to ensure that Contoso's assets and intellectual property are well protected.

3. Is compatible with other existing systems and tools.

4. Is reasonably priced.

5. Supports high-throughput operations and parallel processing.

Data Science

Once all the data is collected and stored in a central data store, the Contoso data team will need to have a platform for:

- Cleaning, transforming, and exploring the datasets.

- Collaborating with other business and technical stakeholders to discover patterns and trends.

- Integrating with artificial intelligence frameworks and runtimes to apply machine learning algorithms on the datasets and uncover any patterns.

- Training and operationalizing the new machine learning models that might come out of the work of *the previous integration.*

- Enabling the team to schedule, run, and monitor data pipelines to enable data transformation, cleaning, and integration.

Dashboards and Reports

Developing data analytics solutions can be seen as a continuous conversation between the data practitioners, business stakeholders, and the data itself. It requires continuous refinement and hypothesis testing. Therefore, it is imperative for Contoso's data team to develop and maintain interactive reports and dashboards to communicate their work and the results of their data discovery processes to the business.

The first step in creating such reports and dashboards is coming up with a consistent and common data model that facilitates a common understanding across the organization.

The Solution

The Contoso data team decided to use Microsoft Azure to implement Contoso's analytics solution. Among other things, the Contoso team listed Azure's scalability, compliance, and regional availability in Contoso's regions (Australia and Japan) as the main factors in making this decision. The team also articulated the reasons why each of the chosen Azure services is fit for purpose, as we will see in the next few sections.

Contoso used the refined requirements and brainstorming ideas (from the previous sections) to come up with a design for the solution architecture. The Contoso data team has come up with the following architecture (as shown in *Figure 5.1*):

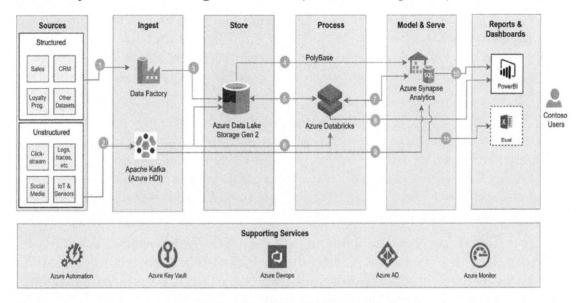

Figure 5.1: Contoso's solution architecture

Data Flow

The design in *Figure 5.1* shows the solution architecture and the data flow between the individual components. Here, we explain each of the workflow segments as marked (numbered) in the preceding diagram:

1. Contoso needs to ingest many varying datasets. Some of these contain structured data and others have unstructured data. For the structured data, Contoso will use **Azure Data Factory** to ingest this data using periodic (5-minute) batch activities and push this data to **Azure Data Lake Storage**.

2. For the unstructured data, Contoso is going to use **Apache Kafka** on an **Azure HDInsight** cluster to capture this data in near real time and push it to both **Azure Data Lake Storage** and **Databricks** (Spark Structured Streaming). This makes all new data available for processing by Contoso's analytics solution and enables Contoso to trigger any action on data in near real time (5-10 seconds behind). The unstructured data includes data coming from clickstream analytics (reports on user behavior on Contoso's digital channels), social media feeds (from Twitter, Facebook, and so on), logs and trace information from Contoso's servers, and any data coming from IoT sensors.

3. Once the data is ingested, **Azure Data Factory** will push the data to **Azure Data Lake Storage**. **Azure Data Factory** has a native data connector to **Azure Data Lake Storage Gen2**.

4. Data that is stored in **Azure Data Lake Storage** can be loaded to the **Azure Synapse Analytics** directly using **PolyBase**. PolyBase is a technology that is developed by Microsoft to unify querying and working with data in SQL servers (and Synapse Analytics) as well as Hadoop-based file systems (such as Azure Data Lake Storage).

5. Contoso's data will land in **Azure Data Lake Storage Gen2**. This data is coming from different sources, with various quality levels and different granularities. Thus, Contoso's data team will need to clean, prepare, validate, and enrich these datasets. This work will be done using **Azure Databricks**. Azure Databricks can connect directly to Azure Data Lake Storage to pull data and store the results of any processed data.

6. Azure Databricks offers the ability to process data streams using Apache Spark Streaming. The Contoso data team will use this to process unstructured data streams that are captured by **Apache Kafka**. Moreover, using Azure HDInsight's native support for **Azure Data Lake Storage Gen2**, incoming data from application logs, social networks, and any other unstructured data will be pushed from **Apache Kafka** to **Azure Data Lake Storage Gen2**. Other structured data streaming can be pushed directly to the **Azure Synapse Analytics** (see *point 9* below).

7. While the Contoso team is cleaning and preparing data in **Azure Databricks**, they will need to pull some data from the **data warehouse** to combine historical data with the newly arriving data. Once all the data preparation is done, the data is then pushed to the **Azure Synapse Analytics** where all data is then combined, modeled, and prepared for consumption. Moreover, Azure Synapse Analytics can be used as an output sink for Apache Spark Structured Streaming. This gives Contoso's downstream users and data analysts the tools to access to the data streams in near real time using the Synapse Analytics. This not only enables Contoso users' systems to run queries and answer questions about the newly arriving data but also combine this new data with the historical data that is already in the Azure Synapse Analytics to come to a consensus about business performance and customer behaviors.

8. **Power BI** can be used to run ad hoc queries over data that is being cleaned and processed in **Azure Databricks**. Power BI supports this integration in multiple ways, including **dataflows**, **Direct Query**, and **data import**.

9. Using Azure Synapse Analytics's new capabilities of handling live data streaming, we can push semi-structured streaming data directly from **Apache Kafka** (HDInsight Cluster) to the **Azure Synapse Analytics**.

10. Power BI enables Contoso not only to publish reports and dashboards for Contoso users, but it also enables every user to be a data analyst for their domain using a self-service approach and by exploring the published data models. Contoso can use composite data models for large data sets which is a feature of Power BI Premium.

11. Contoso invested in complex models using **Microsoft Excel**. Some of Contoso's data analysts would like to use **Microsoft Excel** to access data from the Azure Synapse Analytics. This is supported out of the box in both Microsoft Excel and Azure Synapse Analytics.

Azure Services

The following sections will elaborate on each of the Azure services that are shown in the solution design of *Figure 5.1*. For each service, it will first explain why this component is needed, then why Azure services are fit for purpose for Contoso, and then finally show a brief practical example of the core part of the implementation.

Azure Data Factory

Role in the Design: Contoso, like most other enterprises, has a large number of data sources. Some of these data sources reside on-premises, while some others are on the cloud. As discussed above, Contoso needs to bring all this data together in one place to be able to combine, correlate, model, and transform these datasets to discover trends and insights. This requires building and managing many data connectors to move the data from Contoso's source systems to the central data store (the data lake). This is exactly where Azure Data Factory shines because it is a managed service that is aimed at simplifying data integration for users of all skill levels.

Why Azure Data Factory?

1. Azure Data Factory offers more than 80 pre-built data connectors. This enables Contoso to connect source systems to this new modern data warehouse quickly and easily at no extra cost. These data connectors are built by Microsoft; they offer efficient and resilient integration, and they take advantage of the Microsoft Azure network, which delivers up to 1.5 GB/s in throughput. This not only offers Contoso fast time to market but also provides a platform for orchestrating data movement with minimal overhead.

2. Contoso has a number of existing SQL servers. These servers host a number of **SQL Server Integration Services** (**SSIS**) packages for existing reporting and dashboards. Azure Data Factory offers an integration runtime that is designed to handle SSIS packages. This makes Azure Data Factory a perfect platform for Contoso since it enables Contoso to take advantage of its existing investments in these SSIS packages.

3. Besides all the pre-built data connectors, Azure Data Factory provides a visual interface that empowers everybody to develop comprehensive data movement pipelines with little or no code. Moreover, Azure Data Factory's Visual Editor offers the ability to integrate with Git source control repositories to improve flexibility and maintainability. This resonates well with the Contoso team as it improves their productivity and development pace, while at the same time reducing overhead. Using this feature allows the Contoso team to take advantage of Azure Data Factory's powerful visual data transformation capabilities and data wrangling in the visual portal, while keeping all the work version controlled.

4. Azure Data Factory is a fully managed tool that enables the Contoso team to start small with little or no investment and to scale as needed. This also means that there is no infrastructure to manage, and the Contoso team pays only for what they use.

5. Besides other certifications, Azure Data Factory is **ISO/IEC 27001** and **27018** certified and is available in 25 countries/regions, including Australia and Japan, which is where Contoso operates. This makes Azure Data Factory a very compelling service for Contoso as it ticks all the boxes on their security and compliance checklist.

6. Azure Data Factory provides the tools to build data pipelines that are resilient in the face of schema drift. This means when the Contoso team builds pipelines to move data from source A to B, they can be assured that the pipelines will still be functional, even if the scheme of the data from source A has changed. This significantly improves the reliability and resilience of Contoso's data pipelines.

7. Finally, using Azure Data Factory provides Contoso with a single control plane to manage all activities of data movement and processing.

Sample Implementation

Here is an example of how Contoso configures their Azure Data Factory to pull data from their Sales transactional database (which sits on an Azure SQL server) to Azure Data Lake Storage Gen2:

1. As explained in *Chapter 2, Building Your Modern Data Warehouse*, Azure Data Factory provides native integration with Azure Data Lake Storage Gen2. Contoso can connect to Azure Data Lake Storage Gen2 by configuring a linked service in Azure Data Factory as follows:

```json
{
    "name": "ContosoAzureDLStorageLS",
    "properties": {
        "type": "AzureBlobFS",
        "typeProperties": {
            "url": "https://{accountname}.dfs.core.windows.net",
            "accountkey": {
                "type": "SecureString",
                "value": "{accountkey}"
            }
        },
        "connectVia": {
            "referenceName": "{name of Integration Runtime}",
            "type": "IntegrationRuntimeReference"
        }
    }
}
```

It's worth mentioning that this example contains placeholders for the main configuration values, such as the Azure Storage account **name**, **accountKey**, and the name of the integration runtime.

2. After creating a Linked Service in Azure Data Factory, we need to have an Azure dataset to reference this linked service. This can be done as follows:

```
{
    "name": "ContosoAzureDataLakeSalesDataset",
    "properties": {
        "type": "DelimitedText",
        "linkedServiceName": {
            "referenceName": "ContosoAzureDLStorageLS",
            "type": "LinkedServiceReference"
        },
        "schema": [ { optional } ],
        "typeProperties": {
            "location": {
                "type": "AzureBlobFSLocation",
                "fileSystem": "{filesystemname}",
                "folderPath": "contoso/sales"
            },
            "columnDelimiter": ",",
            "quoteChar": "\"",
            "firstRowAsHeader": true,
            "compressionCodec": "gzip"
        }
    }
}
```

The preceding code snippet makes use of the Azure Data Lake Storage linked service to create a dataset. This dataset will create Comma-Separated Values (CSV) files and store them as compressed files (gzip).

3. Configure the Azure SQL database as a linked service:

```
{
    "name": "ContosoSalesAzureSqlDbLS",
    "properties": {
        "type": "AzureSqlDatabase",
        "typeProperties": {
            "connectionString": {
                "type": "SecureString",
```

```
                     "value": "Server=tcp:{servername}.
    database.windows.net,1433;Database={databasename};User
    ID={username}@{servername};Password={password};Trusted_
    Connection=False;Encrypt=True;Connection Timeout=30"
                 }
         },
         "connectVia": {
             "referenceName": "{name of Integration Runtime}",
             "type": "IntegrationRuntimeReference"
         }
     }
 }
```

Again, the preceding code snippet has placeholders for the following parameters: the Azure SQL Server name, the SQL database name, the SQL server username and password, and the name of the Integration Runtime. Also, the example is for demo purposes only: passwords should always be kept out of the code and should be stored in Azure Key Vault to ensure security.

4. Similar to *step 2*, you need to configure a dataset in Azure Data Factory for Contoso's Sales database. The following code snippet makes use of the Azure SQL Database linked service to create a dataset that references **sales_table** in Contoso's SQL database:

```
{
    "name": "ContosoSalesDataset",
    "properties":
    {
        "type": "AzureSqlTable",
        "linkedServiceName": {
            "referenceName": "ContosoSalesAzureSqlDbLS",
            "type": "LinkedServiceReference"
        },
        "schema": [ {optional} ],
        "typeProperties": {
            "tableName": "sales_table"
        }
    }
}
```

5. The following code snippet configures the data movement activity from the Sales SQL database to Azure Data Lake. This will create an activity in Azure Data Factory and it references the two datasets we created in *step 2* and *step 4*. The activity sets the Azure SQL sales database as the source of the data movement and Azure Data Lake Storage as the destination of the data movement activity:

```
{
    "name": "CopyFromAzureSQLSalesDatabaseToAzureDataLake",
    "type": "Copy",
    "inputs": [
        {
            "referenceName": "ContosoSalesDataset",
            "type": "DatasetReference"
        }
    ],
    "outputs": [
        {
            "referenceName": "ContosoAzureDataLakeSalesDataset",
            "type": "DatasetReference"
        }
    ],
    "typeProperties": {
        "source": {
            "type": "AzureSqlSource",
            "sqlReaderQuery": "SELECT * FROM SALES_TABLE"
        },
        "sink": {
            "type": "ParquetSink",
            "storeSettings":{
                "type": "AzureBlobFSWriteSetting",
                "copyBehavior": "PreserveHierarchy"
            }
        }
    }
}
```

Apache Kafka on Azure HDInsight

Role in the Design

Contoso needs to ingest unstructured streams of data, which could come from applications clickstreams, social media feeds, and IoT devices. This requires a resilient and scalable engine to capture and process these streams as they arrive.

Apache Kafka is a distributed streaming platform that enables the ingestion of data streams from a variety of sources, and it offers a publish-subscribe model to record and transfer data streams. Apache Kafka is a very popular open source project that is used in building real-time streaming applications, which is how Contoso aims to use it. Apache Kafka runs as a cluster, which means Contoso needs a cluster of machines with Apache Kafka installed to be able to use it. This approach is costly, not scalable, and requires lots of maintenance.

Fortunately, Microsoft Azure offers a managed HDInsight cluster to run Apache Kafka in an easy and cost-effective way while at the same time taking advantage of Azure's enterprise-grade **service level agreements** (**SLAs**).

Why Apache Kafka on Azure HDInsight?

As mentioned earlier, Azure HDInsight enables Contoso to easily and quickly run Apache Kafka without having to manage any clusters. Contoso considered the following when deciding on Azure HDInsight for Apache Kafka:

- Azure HDInsight is very easy to set up and get started with. Generally speaking, clusters are hard to set up and manage. Having Microsoft Azure manage the cluster takes away the pain and leaves the Contoso team to focus on solving business problems rather than worrying about infrastructure.

- Contoso pays close attention to security and compliance. Azure HDInsight offers enterprise-grade security controls and has achieved more than 30 compliance certifications.

- Azure HDInsight is built on top of open source technologies and is optimized for Hadoop and Spark. This means that Contoso can run other popular big data solutions on the same cluster (besides Apache Kafka). This makes Contoso's investment more worthwhile as the same cluster can be used to run multiple open source frameworks.

- Besides being easy to set up and manage, Azure HDInsight clusters are also very cost-effective because Contoso can spin up clusters on demand and scale up or down as needed. This means that Contoso does not have to worry about managing or paying for an idle cluster and only needs to pay for what is used.

- Furthermore, Azure HDInsight can be used to analyze and report statistics on big data availability and utilization. Azure HDInsight enables Contoso to use productive tools for Hadoop and Sparks with any preferred development environment.

Sample Implementation

Here is an example of ingesting a data stream in Azure HDInsight (Apache Kafka) and writing it into a compressed Parquet file.

```
// Reading a kafka stream to a dataframe
val kafkaStreamDF = spark.readStream.format("kafka")
                .option("kafka.bootstrap.servers", kafkaBrokers)
                .option("subscribe", kafkaTopic)
                .option("startingOffsets", "earliest")
                .load()
// Writing streaming data to a parquet file
kafkaStreamDF.select(from_json(col("value")
            .cast("string"), schema) as "tweet")
            .writeStream
            .format("parquet")
            .option("path","/contoso/socialmedia/twitterfeed")
            .start.awaitTermination(10000)
```

The preceding code snippet reads the data stream from Apache Kafka into a DataFrame in Scala based on the configuration of Apache Kafka's server and topic. The DataFrame is then written to a compressed (Parquet) file using the provided path with an auto-termination of the job after **10000** seconds. The code snippet also assumes that the Spark libraries for Kafka are installed and referenced properly and that they match the version of Spark on the HDInsight cluster.

Azure Data Lake Storage Gen2

Role in the Design

Azure Data Lake Storage works as Contoso's central data store. This enables Contoso to bring massive amounts of data from varying sources together. Moreover, the type and format of Contoso's datasets vary significantly (structured, semi-structured, and unstructured), which requires a more capable data store than mere tabular storage, which is where Azure Data Lake Storage is needed. Azure Data Lake Storage can store schema-less data as blobs and can handle varying formats (for instance, text files, images, videos, social media feeds, zipped files, and so on). The ability to handle schema-less data formats makes it easy for Contoso to ingest data in its raw format, which is essential for advanced analytics as analysis can be done on the original data without any bias from any data aggregation.

Furthermore, the Contoso team needs elastic storage for a sandbox environment to explore and transform the data. Azure Data Lake Storage can be used for this, too.

Why Azure Data Lake Storage Gen2?

- Contoso uses Azure Active Directory for access management. The Azure Data Lake Storage Gen2 offers native and out-of-the-box integration with Azure Active Directory to manage access to data using Azure Active Directory as the enterprise control mechanism. This reduces the design complexity and improves security and compliance.

- Azure Data Lake Storage Gen2 makes it easier to manage and organize data using directories and subdirectories that are integrated with hierarchical namespaces. This improves performance since it reduces the need to copy or transform data across multiple folders and at the same time it simplifies data management.

- Azure Data Lake Storage Gen2 is built on top of Azure Blob storage, which is designed for low-cost storage. Azure Data Lake Storage Gen2 offers a number of value-adding features, such as hierarchical namespaces, which further reduces the total cost of ownership.

- Besides being low in cost, Azure Data Lake Storage imposes no limits on how much data can be stored. This means that the Contoso team can start small with very minimal costs and scale as needed without worrying about hitting any maximum limits.

- Azure Data Lake Storage integrates natively with Azure Synapse Analytics, Data Factory, Power BI, and many other Microsoft Azure services. This makes a compelling case for the Contoso team since they are already using Power BI and Data Factory.

- Besides integrating with Azure Active Directory, Azure Data Lake Storage Gen2 offers the security features that Contoso's security team demands. This includes data encryption—at rest and in transit—single sign-on, multi-factor authentication, fine-grained access control for users and groups, and full auditing compliance by monitoring every access and configuration change on the data lake.

Sample Implementation

When ingesting data into Azure Data Lake Storage, it is considered a good practice to use namespaces and containers to organize the data in the data lake. This not only makes finding data easier, but it also helps with access control management. *Figure 5.2* shows an example of simple data lake zoning where a data lake is divided into four zones: **Landing Zone** (ingestion), **Staging Zone**, **Secure Zone**, and **Analytics Sandbox**:

- **Landing Zone**: This is where all data (except sensitive data) coming to the data lake will land before being processed, cleaned, aggregated, and so on.

- **Staging Zone**: This is where data will be cleaned/staged before being made ready for consumption.

- **Analytics Sandbox**: This zone is used by data scientists and data engineers as their sandbox for storing data while they are processing and exploring.

- **Secure Zone**: This is where highly sensitive data is stored and processed. Splitting the secure zone from the other zones can enhance access control management. This zone includes sensitive data such as merger and acquisitions data, financial data, and other customer data that might be hard to mask, such as customer gender, age, and ethnicity data, if known:

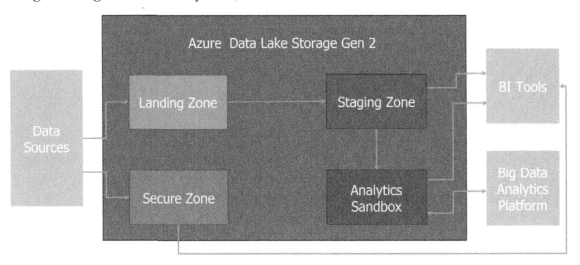

Figure 5.2: Example of data lake storage zoning

Azure Databricks

Role in the Design

Innovation requires meaningful collaboration between data practitioners, developers, and the business. It also requires collecting, cleaning, combining, and transforming big datasets. Databricks is built to enable this collaboration and provide a unified data analytics platform. Contoso will use Azure Databricks as a unified platform for data science and data engineering. Azure Databricks provides the compute power to clean and analyze data, and it supports multiple programming languages and frameworks for varying workloads.

Why Azure Databricks?

- Azure Databricks offers a fully managed Spark cluster, which is what the Contoso team needs for data preparation, transformation, and analysis. Azure Databricks reduces the complexity of deploying and managing the Spark cluster while offering Contoso the ability to get up and running quickly and easily.

- Azure Databricks integrates natively with other Azure services. This is especially important for security and performance. Azure Databricks integrates with Azure Active Directory, which means no new user accounts to be added or managed. Similarly, Azure Databricks supports Azure Synapse Analytics as an output sink for Spark Structured Streaming. This enables Contoso to push new data to its Azure Synapse Analytics in near real time.

- Azure Databricks provides a rich collaboration environment where multiple Contoso stakeholders can work on the same notebook at the same time. This significantly improves productivity and fosters greater innovation by bringing the knowledge of all team members together.

- Azure Databricks enables cluster auto-scaling and auto-termination. This means that Contoso will only need to pay for the cluster when it is in use. This significantly reduces costs by ensuring that the cluster nodes are only running when there is a need for them to run, while at the same time providing greater flexibility by enabling the cluster to scale automatically.

- Diversity is good for innovation, and so Azure Databricks supports multiple programming languages and frameworks. Data scientists and data engineers at Contoso can use R, Python, SQL, Scala, Java, and C# to write code in Azure Databricks. This is especially important for Contoso where it has been hard to recruit and retain talent in this area.

Sample Implementation

Here is a brief sample of Python code that pulls data from the data lake into a
DataFrame:

```
configs = {"fs.azure.account.auth.type": "OAuth",

        "fs.azure.account.oauth.provider.type": "org.apache.hadoop.fs.azurebfs.
oauth2.ClientCredsTokenProvider",

        "fs.azure.account.oauth2.client.id": "{appId}",

        "fs.azure.account.oauth2.client.secret": "{password}",

        "fs.azure.account.oauth2.client.endpoint": "https://login.
microsoftonline.com/{tenant}/oauth2/token",

        "fs.azure.createRemoteFileSystemDuringInitialization": "true"}


dbutils.fs.mount(

source = "abfss://{file-system-name}@{storage-account-name}.dfs.core.windows.
net/folder1",

mount_point = "/mnt/contoso/sales",

extra_configs = configs)


salesDF = spark.read.format('csv').options(
    header='true', inferschema='true').load("/mnt/contoso/sales/*.csv")
```

This code snippet assumes that we have a service principal that is configured with the
right access level in Azure Active Directory. It also has placeholders for the service
principal **appId**, the service principal password, the Azure AD tenant, the Azure Storage
account name, and the Azure Data Lake file system name. Moreover, the code mounts
the Azure Data Lake Storage file system into **/mnt/contoso/sales** and then reads all the
files that have the **.csv** file extension into a Spark DataFrame.

Azure Synapse Analytics

Role in the Design

Contoso needs a single source of truth for all its data. This data needs to be cleaned,
validated, transformed, and aggregated before anything else. Once that is done, this
newly available data needs to be merged with historical datasets so that Contoso can
paint a complete picture of business performance and operations.

Azure Synapse Analytics fills the role of holding the single source of truth. It enables Contoso to create a multi-dimensional model of the data and ensures a well-structured data format that is optimized for querying massive datasets. Furthermore, Contoso also needs a platform where well-curated data is ready for consumption at a predictable performance level. This role is filled by the Azure Synapse Analytics because it separates the data cleaning and validation from the actual data serving.

Why Azure Synapse Analytics?

- Azure Synapse Analytics is a fully managed service and is dynamically scalable. This makes it very attractive for Contoso because it means less infrastructure to manage, less overhead, and a scalable service that can grow with the business.

- Azure Synapse Analytics is 14 times faster than other cloud providers according to an independent benchmark report by GigaOm. Azure SQL provides lightning fast performance for large data volumes. Moreover, Azure Synapse Analytics achieves this via its massively parallel processing capability.

- Azure Synapse Analytics is much cheaper than other cloud products. According to the study by GigaOm, Azure Synapse Analytics is about 94% cheaper than other cloud providers.

- Azure Synapse Analytics has out-of-the-box integration with Apache Spark Structured Streaming. This enables Contoso to create reports and dashboards for customer insights in near real time by combining new streaming data with historical data.

- Contoso's security team has a clear requirement that stipulates the need to protect its data assets. The Contoso security team has demanded that the data warehouse must not be publicly accessible on the web. This is natively supported by Azure Synapse Analytics via Azure Virtual Network integration, where the Azure Synapse Analytics is deployed as part of the Contoso network (a virtual private network).

- Contoso also liked the other security features in Azure Synapse Analytics. These include integration with Azure Active Directory, activity auditing, native row and column-based security, ExpressRoute integration, and the out-of-the-box threat detection and data encryption capabilities.

- Some parts of Contoso use other BI tools like Power BI, Tableau, and Qlik and they wanted to make sure that the new data warehouse supports this integration. Azure Synapse Analytics is compatible with many BI tools, including Contoso's existing BI tools.

- Azure Synapse Analytics can also spin up Apache Spark on demand. This can be remarkably useful for Contoso's data team, as it enables them to use the same Open Source tooling to work with their data inside Azure Synapse Analytics. This facilitates better productivity, as Spark clusters support multiple languages and frameworks out of the box (Python, R, Scala, etc).Thus, Contoso's team members can be productive and happy using the tools they are most comfortable with.

- Developing, deploying and managing a Data Warehouse can be a very complex exercise. Azure Synapse Analytics shines in this area, as it draws on Microsoft's wealth of experience as a development company. Part of the reason why Contoso is so interested in Azure Synapse Analytics is its streamlined workload management and excellent developer productivity. Azure Synapse Analytics is the only cloud data warehouse that offers native SSMS and SSDT support, including Visual Studio projects for code and schema management which are vital to ensure a streamlined development lifecycle and reduce Total-Cost-of-Ownership.

Sample Implementation

Azure Synapse Analytics can be used as an output sink for Spark Structured Streaming in Azure Databricks. This offers the ability to bring live streaming data into Azure Synapse Analytics quickly and easily. Here is a brief example of the main steps involved:

1. The following code snippet creates a table called `TweetsStream` in the Azure Synapse Analytics to receive the stream. This table has two simple columns—one for the `timestamp` and one for the `Value` that is received from the data stream. The example below assigns `ROUND_ROBIN` as the distribution policy for this table. Choosing a distribution policy can have a major impact on performance. Generally, choose `HASH-DISTRIBUTED` tables for improving query performance on large fact tables, and choose `ROUND_ROBIN` for improving loading speed:

```
CREATE TABLE [dbo].[TweetsStream]
(
  [timestamp] DATETIME NULL,
  [Value] BIGINT NULL
)
WITH
(
  DISTRIBUTION = ROUND_ROBIN,
  CLUSTERED INDEX ([timestamp])
)
```

2. This next step sets up the Python script on Azure Databricks. The following code snippet uses placeholders for the Azure Synapse Analytics connection details. The code establishes a connection to the Azure Synapse Analytics using **Java Database Connectivity** (**JDBC**). It also sets up an Azure Blob storage account to use for temporary storage:

```python
# Setup the connection to the Azure SQL DW
dwDatabase = {databaseName}
dwServer = {servername}
dwUser = {sqlUser}
dwPass = {password}
dwJdbcPort =  "1433"
dwJdbcExtraOptions =
"encrypt=true;trustServerCertificate=true;loginTimeout=30;"
sqlDwUrl = "jdbc:sqlserver://" + dwServer + ".database.windows.net:" +
dwJdbcPort + ";database=" + dwDatabase + ";user=" + dwUser+";password=" +
dwPass + ";"+dwJdbcExtraOptions

# Setup Blob Storage for temporary storage of the data stream
stAccount = {StorageAccount}
container = {container}
blobAccessKey =  {accessKey}
spark.conf.set("fs.azure.account.key."+blobStorage , blobAccessKey)
```

The following Python code snippet reads the Spark data stream. The code configures the number of rows to be read per second as **4000** rows per second and the number of partitions as **4**:

```python
df = spark.readStream \
  .format("rate") \
  .option("rowsPerSecond", "4000") \
  .option("numPartitions", "4") \
  .load()
```

3. Then you are continuously writing the stream data to the data warehouse table:

```
df.writeStream \
  .format("com.databricks.spark.sqldw") \
  .option("url", sqlDwUrl) \
  .option("tempDir", "wasbs://"+container+"@"+stAccount+"/tmpdir/twts") \
  .option("forwardSparkAzureStorageCredentials", "true") \
  .option("dbTable", "TweetsStream")  \
  .trigger(processingTime="5 seconds") \
  .start()
```

The preceding code snippet will save the data stream to the nominated Azure Storage container temporarily, then PolyBase will pick up the data from the temporary container to the target Azure Synapse Analytics table (`TweetsStream`). The code is set to be triggered every **5 seconds**.

Power BI

Role in the Design

The Contoso team needs to visualize and communicate its findings as well as some of the raw data to the business. This is critical to ensure engagement from the business stakeholders and to get feedback quickly and easily. Contoso also needs a platform to enable users to use self-service reports and dashboards and to empower Contoso users to explore data for themselves.

Power BI fills this role by enabling Contoso to visualize data using a variety of visuals and shapes, and by also enabling business and non-technical users to self-service any reporting and/or data needs.

Why Power BI?

Power BI is a business intelligence **software as a service (SaaS)** offering that allows Contoso to transform its data into interactive visuals and dashboards quickly and easily. Contoso chooses Power BI not just because of its visualization capabilities, but also in an effort to improve collaboration and self-service for data and reporting—core features of the Power BI service. The Contoso data team summarized their rationale for why Power BI is fit for this purpose, as follows:

- Power BI is a fully managed SaaS offering, which means less infrastructure for the Contoso team to manage.

- Power BI has simplified data visualization and reporting, and can empower any Contoso user to be a data analyst. The user experience in Power BI is a major advantage of the platform, and it enables users to explore data and interactive dashboards for themselves. Contoso hopes that this will reduce overhead and data requests for their data team, as well as improve collaboration and business user engagement.

- Power BI provides a desktop application that can be used by Contoso users to explore data, clean data, and create visuals. This is very attractive to Contoso since the use of the Power BI desktop app is free and does not require a commercial license. Moreover, the user experience on the Power BI desktop app and the Power BI cloud-based service is very similar, which means less training and easier knowledge transfer.

- Power BI has native integration with Azure Active Directory, which enables Contoso users to use their existing identities. This simplifies deployments, improves governance, and enhances security. Moreover, Power BI has gone through many compliance certifications and is available in many regions around the world, including Australia, which is where Contoso is based.

- Contoso has well-defined branding and promotional guidelines. This means that all visualizations and dashboards must adhere to Contoso's color styles, best practices, and so on. Contoso believes this improves branding and information comprehension because the reports are consistent and familiar to the user. Power BI supports this requirement by offering a number of features, such as customizable themes, customizable layouts, and other custom visuals.

- Power BI offers out-of-the-box integration with Azure. This enables Contoso to start with any data preparation and transformation locally and scale to Azure when needed. Plus, Power BI has native integration with Azure AI services. This enables Contoso to infuse AI and machine learning capabilities to deliver value more quickly and easily, all from within Power BI.

- Power BI Composite Model enables Contoso to have rich reports that fetch data from multiple sources. Composite Models allows Contoso to seamlessly include data connections from more than one DirectQuery or Import data connection in any combination. This simplifies data connections from reports to the data sources and it helps Contoso to build complex data models by combining multiple source systems and to join tables from different datasets. Moreover, using the Storage Mode feature of Composite models in Power BI Premium can help improve performance and reduce back-end load. This is because Power BI gives the author of a report the ability to specify which visuals require (or not require) back-end data sources. Power BI then caches (stores) the visuals that do not require continuous updates from back-end data sources, which in turn improves performance and reduces load on backend systems.

Sample Implementation

Here is an example of Contoso's dashboards. The following reports aim to communicate Contoso's performance in terms of product sales in their respective categories, the current stock of the top-selling products, sales figures per year, and the regional distribution of Contoso's customers. The report was built using sample data that is provided by Microsoft:

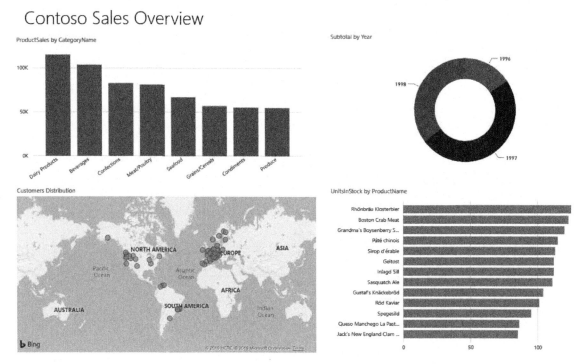

Figure 5:3: An example of Contoso's business performance dashboards

Azure Supporting Services

Besides all the Azure services that have been covered, Contoso needs a number of other services to support and enable this solution architecture. These services are shown in the **Supporting Services** section of the solution design back in *Figure* 5.1. In this section, we briefly describe each of these Azure services.

Azure Automation

Contoso has a number of database servers, test machines, and other supporting servers. Contoso can use Azure Automation to automate the configuration and installation of updates on these machines. Azure Automation enables Contoso to have a consistent way of managing these servers and ensures security and compliance using serverless runbooks. This simplifies the operations and management overhead and gives the Contoso team time back to focus on the more important issue, which is discovering insights that add business value.

Azure Key Vault

Every organization has many encryption keys, passwords, certificates, connection strings, and other sensitive data that needs to be well secured. Contoso understands the need to protect this sensitive information and manage it in a secure and well-organized way. Azure Key Vault is designed to solve exactly this problem by safeguarding all such sensitive data in a central place where access can be securely managed, and keys can be organized. Azure Key Vault not only improves security controls but also simplifies operational tasks such as certificate and key rotation.

Moreover, Contoso wants to use Azure Key Vault to remove the need for individuals and applications to have direct access to keys. Contoso can use Azure's Managed Service Identity so that users and applications can use keys and passwords without having to keep any local copies on their machines. This improves the overall security posture of Contoso while at the same time streamlining secret management.

Azure DevOps

Azure DevOps provides Contoso with the tools, frameworks, and services to run an agile practice to deliver its solution. Azure DevOps is a fully managed service that empowers the Contoso team to:

- Plan, track, discuss, and monitor work items using Azure Boards. Contoso is already using agile practices, where currently physical walls are used to track work items, but Contoso realizes that physical walls cannot scale for bigger teams and they are limited in their functionality. For instance, Contoso can use Azure Boards to link defects and work items to code changes to monitor and improve code quality.

- Continuously build, test, and deploy code changes using Azure Pipelines. Azure Pipelines facilitate agile practices such as continuous integration and continuous delivery, which can significantly improve the quality and pace of delivery. Azure Pipelines also allow Contoso to automate any deployment steps that are needed to push code changes. This reduces overhead and improves confidence in the new deployments.

- Contoso needs a source control system to host its code and scripts. Contoso would like to use Azure Repos for this as it provides enterprise-grade support, an unlimited number of repositories, and a collaborative environment for the development team to discuss and review code changes before merging.

- Azure Test Plans can help Contoso in the validation and verification of any code and data changes to give Contoso greater confidence in changes before merging them. Contoso can use Azure Test Plans for manual as well as exploratory testing, and since Azure Test Plans is part of Azure DevOps, Contoso can have great end-to-end traceability for stories, features, and defects.

Azure Active Directory

Contoso uses Microsoft Office 365 for office collaboration, which means Contoso is already using Azure Active Directory. Contoso does not want to have multiple identity servers to manage and it understands that managing usernames and passwords is a massive task that is better left to a well-equipped team, such as the Active Directory team. Azure Active Directory has integration with many of the services that Contoso is aiming to use, such as SQL Server, Azure Synapse Analytics, Azure Data Lake Storage, and Power BI. This makes it a no-brainer for Contoso to choose Azure Active Directory to enable simple and seamless login to all these services while at the same time improving security controls over Contoso's data and applications.

Contoso can also benefit from Azure Active Directory's comprehensive identity protection, which includes threat detection and response. Overall, Contoso can reduce overhead remarkably and improve security by using Azure Active Directory.

Azure Monitor

Contoso recognizes that the availability and performance of its data platform is of paramount importance to gain the confidence and trust of all stakeholders. To achieve that, Contoso not only needs to collect and store telemetry from all solution areas but also analyze and action any data. This requires a dedicated service since it is a major challenge to implement, and that is exactly what Azure Monitor is designed for.

Azure Monitor is a fully managed service that empowers Contoso to easily and quickly collect, analyze, and action data from all components of the data platform (including Azure services, virtual machines, network performance, and other sources). Azure Monitor offers two fundamental types of data, which are logs and metrics. Contoso can use metrics to learn about the state of its services at any given time, while the logs help the Contoso team analyze and visualize trace messages from the individual solution components. Azure Monitor also offers a large number of charts and visualizations that can be used by Contoso to visualize the state of the system at a glance. Finally, Contoso can use Azure Monitor to trigger actions such as alerts when certain conditions are met (for instance, when the number of errors goes beyond a certain threshold, the Contoso team can be notified by email or SMS).

Insights and Actions

Using Microsoft Azure, the Contoso data team was able to design, build, and deploy the solution quickly and easily. Within two weeks, the team found a number of key insights that can help Contoso increase profit margin. Three of these insights are listed below.

Reducing Waste by 18%

Description: With initial modeling, the Contoso data team was able to reduce waste by 18%. Currently, the organization loses close to $46M per year because of overstocking products with short shelf lives. This includes products such as bread and milk. The team combined historical sales data with other sources, such as weather data and school calendars, which allowed the team to predict the demand for these products with higher accuracy leading to a significant reduction in waste.

Estimated Business Value: $8.28M/year

Key Data Sources: Sales transactions (online and physical store), store data (store locations and stock over time), weather data, suburb profile data, school calendars, and public holiday calendar.

Actions: Business stakeholders of Contoso were very impressed and wanted to deploy this quickly. Using Azure Synapse Analytics and Power BI, the Contoso data team was able to deploy the solution for use by store managers quickly. The result is that Contoso's store managers now have an interactive dashboard that can predict sales accurately and give recommendations for the amount of stock to have for each product.

Data Pipeline: Here is the simplified data pipeline for this initiative:

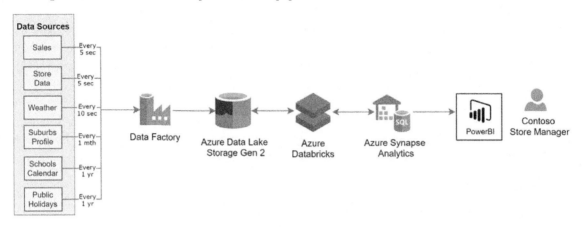

Figure 5.4: Data pipeline for initiative 1 (reducing waste)

Social Media Trends Drive Sales up by 14%

Description: The Contoso data team developed a hypothesis that social media trends can increase sales. The team performed initial data discovery to find that such a pattern does indeed exist. Interestingly, the team discovered that timing Contoso's marketing activities with social media trends can help Contoso improve sales by 14%.

One clear example of this was what the team found in the data of Australia's summer season of 2017. In Jan 2017, there was a huge social media trend related to healthy eating. This was not organized by Contoso. There were more than 4.5M Australians who tweeted, liked, shared, or commented on Twitter and Facebook posts using the **#BeHealthy** hashtag. Coincidentally, Contoso had a marketing campaign regarding fruit salad products. The team found that this marketing campaign was exceptionally successful and increased sales by over 25%, which is much higher than the average expected increase of 5-10%.

Estimated Business Value: $15.4M/year (based on 14% increase for subject products)

Key Data Sources: Social media feeds (Twitter, Facebook, and Instagram), sales transactions (online and physical store), store data (store locations and stock over time), and marketing campaign data.

Actions: After discussing the results with the Contoso marketing team, it was agreed that Contoso could reproduce the success of their Jan 2017 promotion by monitoring and aligning their promotions with social media trends. The Contoso data team implemented the data pipeline, as shown in the following screenshot, and deployed it as an interactive and real-time dashboard to inform both the Contoso marketing team and store managers.

Data Pipeline: Here is the simplified data pipeline for this initiative:

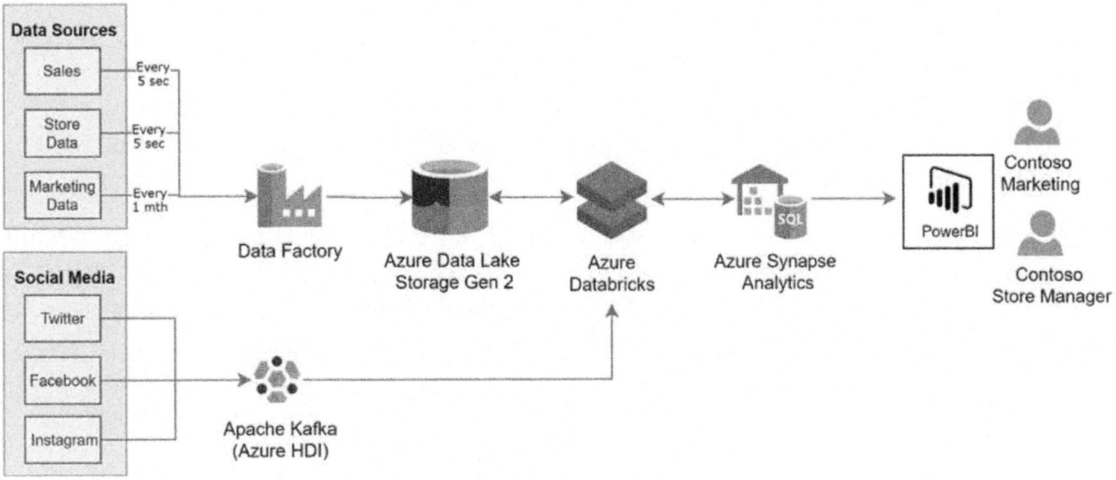

Figure 5.5: Data pipeline for initiative 2 (increasing sales)

Conclusion

You have seen how Contoso (or any other organization) can take advantage of Microsoft Azure to discover customer insights and add value in near real time. Microsoft Azure offers a wide range of services for data management and analytics and aims to streamline the development process while at the same time raising the bar for quality and performance.

Furthermore, Microsoft Azure offers many data and analytics services as fully managed offerings, which means less overhead for Contoso (and any other organization). The other advantage of using serverless Azure is that organizations and teams can start small with no major investment and scale up as demand grows. This is a great business approach as it reduces the risks of upfront investment, while at the same time mitigating the burden of bureaucratic approval for large expenditure at the start of a data project.

Finally, Microsoft Azure provides a great deal of documentation and learning materials online and aims to break the barrier to entry by offering free credit that can be used by any team or individual to start learning and building with Azure today.

Use Case 2: Using Advanced Analytics on Azure to Create a Smart Airport

Najad is a large city in the northern part of Egypt. The city's main airport, Najad International Airport (NIA), services 25 million passengers per year, which amounts to 70,000 passengers every day. It is Egypt's busiest airport and sees an average of 200,000 flights every year.

The management of NIA is hoping to adopt data analytics on Azure to improve capacity planning and quality of service. The goal is to use data to address operational issues that are currently hindering NIA's ability to fully utilize its infrastructure and resources. This will, in turn, improve customer satisfaction and enable NIA to scale its operation by serving more passengers and airplanes.

The following sections will define the problems that NIA is facing and brainstorm some design ideas. Finally, you will create a possible solution architecture on Microsoft Azure that can solve this problem and explain why Azure is the perfect platform for such solutions.

The Problem

To properly define the business problem, you first need to consider the challenges from the business perspective. Then you will look at the technical problems hindering the airport's ability to move forward.

Business Challenges

As mentioned, NIA serves tens of millions of passengers every year. The volume of these passengers is forecasted to increase by about 20% in the next 3-5 years. Last year, the airport suffered a loss of more than $370M due to operational inefficiencies. This included costs of flight delays due to congestion and long queues, lost retail opportunities due to poor passenger experience, poor planning of staffing levels, and under-utilization of airport assets.

NIA's CIO, Zara Hassan, is relatively new (she's only been with NIA for 6 months) and has a background in data and business intelligence. Zara has a vision for turning this massive inefficiency at NIA into a business opportunity. She presented a business case to the NIA board to make small incremental investments in advanced analytics in order to reduce the airport's overall operational costs, while at the same time improving customer experience.

As a visionary, Zara understands that for the airport to succeed, it has to move from observing historical reports to predicting the future. She wants her team to help the airport management predict flight delays and mitigate such occurrences. She believes that if the airport management has access to the right tools, then capacity planning, resource allocation, and safety can all be improved.

The proposed approach is to use data and artificial intelligence to model passengers, flights, baggage, assets, and other datasets to be able to confidently predict passenger volume and crowd movement, which in turn will allow the airport to improve its operations and reduce costs.

The business challenges faced by the NIA data analytics team can be summarized as follows:

- The first major challenge for the airport's management is to improve capacity planning. Currently, the leadership team at NIA makes these decisions based on assumptions and previous experiences, which does not necessarily reflect reality. So far, NIA has not had a consistent data-driven approach to predict the number of passengers they can expect on a given day. Accuracy in predicting the number of expected passengers is critical for capacity planning such as managing staffing levels and the purchase of equipment, as well as the planning of infrastructure upgrades. Moreover, NIA does not have a solution in place to predict the airlines that might get delayed or predict the number of security personnel the airport might need on a given day to serve passengers. This leads to overcrowding, long queues, and inefficient infrastructure utilization. Poor capacity planning alone was estimated to have cost NIA close to $160M last year. Add to that new assets such as vehicles and carts that the airport purchased because of the perceived need, while in reality they just needed to improve the utilization of existing assets.

- Resource allocation is another major concern for NIA's management. The passengers have to wait at the airport in long queues, whether at customs or at the airlines' check-in counters. Most of these long waits are due to the poor allocation of NIA staff to different areas of the airport. NIA's management wants to improve resource allocation, which would then improve customer satisfaction.

- The retail and duty-free shops at the airport make up a decent portion of the airport's revenue. NIA has a number of large billboards, and they use customer information to provide some occasional promotions. The NIA management would like to improve customer engagement and eventually business opportunities at these airport retail shops.

- A big part of customer service is to provide customers with the information they need when they need it. Traveling through an airport can be a very tiring experience, and it can also be stressful when passengers are running late or have a flight delayed or canceled. NIA thus needs to update the flight status/delays in near real time. This requires NIA's management to think of creative and innovative ways to make the relevant information available to customers when they need it. This will reduce customer confusion and stress and improve the overall customer service.

- NIA needs an infrastructure overhaul in the long term. This would solve the problem of congestion, which has caused minor accidents in the past and has cost the airport money while negatively impacting customer experience. However, NIA is looking to improve passenger flow and reduce congestion by making proper use of resources as a short-term solution for the near future. Congestion hampers the flow of passengers and creates safety hazards when too many people are forced to go through small halls and/or walkways, especially when there are old people, babies, and disabled passengers. This creates safety incidents, and each of these safety alerts and incidents costs the airport money, puts the lives of passengers at risk, and negatively impacts the customer experience. The airport wants to improve passenger flow to reduce congestion and improve safety.

Now that you know the main pain points that the business side of NIA is hoping to address, you'll need to consider the technical challenges so that you can start designing a solution.

Technical Challenges

No single source of truth: One main problem that NIA's CIO is trying to solve is the fact that NIA currently has no single source of truth in terms of data sources. Today, the airport relies on reports from a number of old internal systems, as well as reports from partners. These reports usually cover operational aspects of the previous day and week and have conflicting figures. For instance, flight data currently is held by the individual carrier companies. NIA has more than 35 airline companies, each of which has its own systems and uses different terminologies. This makes it extremely difficult for the NIA management to get credible reports in time, let alone have data-driven operations.

Latency in obtaining data and reports: Because NIA does not have control over flight and cargo data, it relies on partners to generate, aggregate, and send operational reports. These reports are usually delayed by days or weeks. This significantly reduces the organization's ability to action any insights from these reports and forces NIA to always be reactive in its operations rather than planning ahead. For instance, if a report is presented to the airport management and shows that there were long queues that caused flight delays yesterday, the airport management can't change the situation since it happened in the past. Timely access to this data is critical for NIA and almost all other organizations.

Data availability and access: Innovation requires exploring possibilities and experimenting with options. In terms of data, this requires NIA to continuously explore, enrich, and correlate flight and passenger data with external data sources. Unfortunately, NIA cannot do any of these today because the data is sitting in many silo systems that the airport does not control.

Scalability: NIA currently has a SQL Data Warehouse that is hosted in its virtual data center. The management team has been reluctant to invest in this data warehouse because it does not hold all the data. This makes the current data warehouse obsolete because it does not help the business in finding the insights the airport needs. Moreover, this current SQL Data Warehouse does not have the ability to ingest and/or hold all data that NIA can collect.

Security: NIA has clear and strict policies to protect its data and all of its customers' data. The airport is required to clear ISO/IEC 27001 and ISO/IEC 27018 certifications to ensure that security measures are properly applied to protect the airport, its suppliers, its customers, and all stakeholders. NIA needs to ensure all these security requirements in any potential solution.

Data service-ability: For any data to be useful, it needs to be provided to the relevant users at the right time. NIA currently serves notices and alarms to passengers using audio announcements as well as a few large monitors placed in a few locations around the airport. This is highly inefficient because it creates noise and it does not take into account the context of who the user is or what the user wants to know. NIA now acknowledges that it needs to raise its game not only in improving data and report efficacy but also in how these reports are served to users.

Based on these requirements, NIA's business intelligence team, along with the CIO, agree to define the problem statement as follows:

NIA is losing more than $350M a year because of operational inefficiencies, which include long queues, poor staffing levels, and under-utilization of airport assets. The NIA business intelligence team will work to deliver data analytics tools (dashboards, reports, and apps) that help the business optimize operations and remove inefficiencies.

Design Brainstorming

After defining the problem and articulating the business and technical challenges, the next few sections will help you to brainstorm some design ideas to come up with a solution design for NIA.

Data Sources

Data is at the center of any analytics solution. Hence, you need to start by thinking about the different types of data that NIA would need. Then, you need to think about a design to bring this data together. NIA needs to collect data from the following sources:

- **Customs data**: Customs data holds information about passengers and their declarations as they enter or leave the country. Currently, customs data is held by external systems. However, the airport can pull this data and integrate it into its systems. The current mechanism of integrating with the customs data system is using a scheduled file dump to a file server. This can be used by NIA to pull customs data to its new platform.

- **Airline/flights data**: Currently, the individual airline systems hold the passenger data, their trips, check-in times, and other related details. Although this data is held by the airline systems, the airport can integrate with these systems using integration APIs. The specific implementation of this integration will vary based on the individual airlines, but the airport needs to obtain this data in near real time.

- **Parking systems data**: The airport has sensors at all parking facilities that count cars coming in and going out. The parking systems also have an indication at any given point of how many parking spaces are available and where. This data will need to be ingested with other sources.

- **IoT and video streams**: NIA has a number of traffic-monitoring cameras that are installed throughout the site. These cameras send live video streaming and are used by the control room to direct resources and adapt operational procedures to cope with the traffic. The airport also has IoT sensors installed near the gates to indicate the status of each gate. There are also sensors that are aimed at monitoring crowd distribution in the airport. Data from all these sources (IoT and cameras) can be streamed for real-time analysis to provide NIA's management with actionable insights as traffic issues arise.

- **Baggage systems data**: The airport has an internal system that is used to manage all baggage data. This includes what luggage has arrived, on which flight, and where it is now. The airport also serves logistics companies and receives multiple cargo flights every day. It is important to collect and analyze all the relevant data to serve these logistics companies for freight management.

- **Social media feeds**: In order to provide good customer service, it is essential for NIA to analyze passenger sentiment and feedback as passengers are expected to use social media platforms to share their experiences. This helps NIA to improve its services and address any concerning issues immediately.

- **Other data sources**: As discussed in *Use case 1*, it is very common in data analytics to enrich existing datasets with other external sources of data to provide more context to any trends or patterns that are found. This is especially true for airport operations where things can be heavily impacted by weather data, holiday seasons, and other such factors. NIA will need to ingest many of these external data sources to complement its own operational data.

Data Storage

The airport estimates its current existing data to be close to 310 TB, which does not include all the partners' data that needs to be collected and stored. To add to that, the airport is aiming to pull camera streaming as well as social media feeds. This could add an extra 15 GB of data per day based on historical figures. This requires a highly scalable data storage service that can adapt elastically to the rapidly increasing volumes.

To address this requirement, it makes sense to use a cloud-based service such as Azure Data Lake Storage to ensure elastic scalability and the ability to store data in various formats.

Data Ingestion

To ensure that data is made available to the airport staff and customers in a timely manner, data needs to be ingested from internal and external sources quickly and efficiently. Based on the data sources that have been discussed, the solution needs to cater to multiple forms of data ingestion. This includes loading file dumps, processing real-time data streams from social media and monitoring cameras, and pulling data by calling to external APIs. The data team at NIA can either build their own integration and ingestion solution, which would be very expensive and would require plenty of development time, or use a cloud-based data ingestion and orchestration tool such as Azure Data Factory (ADF). ADF streamlines the data ingestion process by offering more than 80 pre-built data connectors, which can be used to integrate with a variety of source systems such as SQL databases, blob storage, and flat files.

Security and Access Control

The solution needs to provide the right security controls to NIA's management so that data can be secured and protected. Understandably, the airport has a long list of stakeholders that need to have access to data, including airport staff, security contractors, airline crew, passengers, and partners. Therefore, the solution needs to enable NIA to provide row-level security to ensure that users only have access to their data. This requires a fine-grained access control management system that is built into the chosen platform so that the NIA business intelligence team does not need to spend too much time worrying about security. The focus of the NIA business intelligence team should be on finding insights that can help the airport management.

Discovering Patterns and Insights

A key part of Zara's strategy is to empower the business to make decisions intelligently. This intelligence is assumed to be acquired by exploring and discovering trends and patterns in data. The major challenge here is where and how to build these machine learning models. Building such models requires working with many large datasets and an elastic pool of compute resources. The team acknowledges the challenge ahead and is looking to use Azure Databricks, which represents the state of the art in analytics platforms. The team was impressed with the scalability, security, and wide support of tools and frameworks on Azure Databricks.

The Solution

The CIO of NIA, with the help of the business intelligence team, agreed to use Microsoft Azure as the cloud provider to build the new solution. They summarized their reasoning as follows.

Why Azure for NIA?

- NIA is already using Microsoft technologies such as Windows 10, Office 365, and other tools. Azure has better native integration with all these services than any other cloud provider. Thus, it makes perfect sense to use Azure. Furthermore, NIA is keen to take advantage of the **Open Data Initiative** (**ODI**), which enables organisations to deliver exceptional business insights by combining behavioral, transactional, financial, and operational data in one data store. The initiative simplifies creating common data models across the organisation and was developed jointly by Adobe, Microsoft, and SAP.

- Using Azure means that NIA can keep using the same centralized Identity server, which is managed using Azure Active Directory for Office 365. This means better security for NIA and less overhead when creating and managing new user accounts.

- Azure has more regional data centers than other major cloud providers. This means that Azure can provide higher resiliency and service availability to NIA. In addition to that, Azure is the only cloud provider that has a regional data center in Africa, which is where NIA is based. This makes Azure the perfect choice as it ticks all the boxes.

- The NIA business intelligence team found that using Azure is more cost-effective than using other cloud providers. Azure's Synapse Analytics (formerly known as SQL Data Warehouse) is 14 times cheaper than AWS or Google services, as explained in *Use case* 1. Moreover, Azure provides the ability to use reserved instances for virtual machines and compute instances, which can give even greater discounts. Furthermore, using NIA's existing enterprise agreement with Microsoft, NIA can get even further discounts on all Azure services retail prices. This makes it very hard to justify choosing any other cloud provider.

- NIA also considered Microsoft's track record in developer technologies and developer experience as a big advantage for Azure. As a software development company, Microsoft provides the best developer experience using its wealth of intellectual property in this field. This means that NIA can have a good development and deployment experience when using Azure.

- Azure has achieved more than 30 compliance certifications, including **ISO/IEC 27001** and **ISO/IEC 27018**, which are also required by NIA. Add to that the fact that the Azure business model is not based on using or selling customer data, which is part of the business model of other cloud providers. This gives greater assurances to NIA and its board that their data and their customers' data is well protected.

- NIA is also hoping to use Azure Stack, which provides the airport with the ability to host applications and services on premises and in the cloud seamlessly using the same base infrastructure, which is powered by Azure and Azure Stack.

- Finally, NIA wants to have the ability to choose a mix of **PaaS**, **SaaS**, and open source tools. Azure enables NIA to do exactly that by offering great PaaS and SaaS services such as Azure Data Lake, Azure Data Factory, and others, while at the same time supporting native integration with open source services such as Databricks and Kafka.

Solution Architecture

Now that the BI team has refined the requirements and a cloud platform has been chosen, it is time to come up with a secure and scalable design. The NIA business intelligence team went with the following solution architecture:

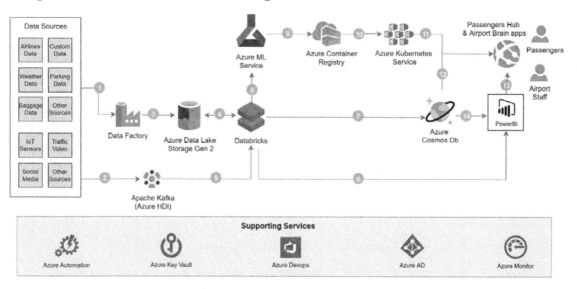

Figure 5.6: Solution architecture for NIA

The design in *Figure* 5.6 shows the solution architecture and the data flow between the individual components. Here's an explanation for each of the workflow segments, as marked (numbered) in the diagram:

1. Structured data such as **Airlines Data**, **Custom Data**, and **Baggage Data** is ingested using **Azure Data Factory**. This includes other data sources, such as data from the parking systems and weather data. Azure Data Factory provides the ability for NIA to configure an integration runtime that can be used as a gateway to connect to NIA's on-premises data sources from within Azure.

2. All unstructured data, including **IoT Sensors** data, **Traffic Video** streaming, and **Social Media** feeds, will be ingested using **Apache Kafka** on an **Azure HDInsight** cluster. Using Apache Kafka here on Azure HDInsight enables NIA to filter and transform incoming data streams as they arrive before ingestion.

3. **Azure Data Factory** pushes the ingested structured data to **Azure Data Lake Storage Gen2** for storage.

4. **Azure Databricks** is used as the unified data analytics platform to enable NIA's data scientists and data engineers to work on cleaning, transforming, and discovering data. Azure Databricks reads the ingested datasets from Azure Data Lake Storage and also uses Data Lake Storage to store any results and curated data.

5. The incoming data stream (from **Social Media** and **IoT Sensors**) is pushed from Kafka to Apache Structured Streaming in Azure Databricks. This enables the business intelligence team to store the incoming data in Azure Data Lake Storage.

6. **Azure Machine Learning Services** is used to manage the machine learning models, datasets, experiments, and new model images. Azure Machine Learning Services has native integration with Azure Databricks.

7. Cleaned data that is ready for consumption is then pushed from Azure Databricks to **Azure Cosmos DB**. This includes the most recent flight data and baggage data to make the data available for consumption by the airport's passengers and staff.

8. **Power BI** is also configured to read more extensive datasets directly from **Azure Databricks**. Examples of the data that will be pushed using this mechanism include the results of decoding the traffic video stream to create crowd heatmaps.

9. Azure Machine Learning Services is used to train and build machine learning models. The resulting models are stored as Docker images in **Azure Container Registry**. Docker images are generally used as a way of packaging machine learning models with all their dependencies (libraries, source code, and configuration files) as one single deployable package. This improves the development life cycle and reduces deployment errors.

10. **Azure Kubernetes Service** is configured with the deployment to take the new machine learning model images from **Azure Container Registry** and run these models as Kubernetes pods. This makes the machine learning models available to generate predictions by making simple HTTP calls. Examples of the machine learning models include a recommendation engine for gate assignments and a parking demand forecasting machine learning model.

11. The NIA business intelligence team can deploy the new machine learning models via web applications, which can be hosted on **Azure Kubernetes Service**. These web applications can then interact with **Azure Cosmos DB** to save machine learning inference data (such as what actions are recommended to the airport staff) as well as to serve curated data such as flight schedule and baggage data. Examples of these web applications are **Passengers Hub** and **Airport Brain**. Passengers Hub is designed to be the one central portal to serve all passengers' data, which includes things such as flight details, gate numbers, check-in counters, and recommendations to the passenger. Passengers can see all this information on their mobile device by downloading the airport's mobile app.

12. Airport Brain is the name given to the new central portal for the airport management staff. The goal is to provide NIA's management with the tools to enable efficient operations. The portal uses data to provide recommendations on gate assignments, staffing levels, and the distribution of airport assets.

13. Both **Passengers Hub** and **Airport Brain** make use of the curated data that is stored in Azure Cosmos DB. Azure Cosmos DB is also used to store application-specific types of data such as users' sessions and alerts. This is all enabled by Azure Cosmos DB's blazing-fast querying engine and high responsiveness.

14. Both **Passengers Hub** and **Airport Brain** require data visualization. Power BI is used to build these reports and then use the web page embedding feature of Power BI to present these Power BI reports on the new web applications. The curated data includes passenger-related information such as passenger flight details, any predicted delays, and passenger baggage info.

15. The Power BI dashboard serves data from Azure Cosmos DB, which includes curated passenger-related data, as listed in *point* 13.

Azure Services

As in *Use case* 1, the following sections will elaborate on each of the Azure services that are shown in *Figure* 5.6. They will first explain why each service is needed, why it is suitable for NIA, and then, finally, show a brief practical example of the core part of its implementation. To avoid repetition, the Azure services that are covered in *Use case* 1 are skipped unless NIA has specific requirements for that service.

Azure Databricks

Role in the Design

Azure Databricks serves as the unified platform for cleaning, transforming, merging, and exploring data. Azure Databricks is needed to provide the compute power needed to process data and to foster greater collaboration between the many stakeholders.

Why Azure Databricks?

Besides all the advantages of Azure Databricks that were covered in *Use case* 1, Azure Databricks supports multiple languages, machine learning frameworks (such as TensorFlow and PyTorch), and integrates with many open source tools. NIA's business intelligence team needs a platform that can handle both data engineering and data science workloads. Azure Databricks is designed to serve this purpose by enabling data engineers to clean, merge, transform, and curate data, while at the same time empowering data scientists to use any of the popular machine learning frameworks, such as TensorFlow or PyTorch.

Sample Implementation

The following code snippet configures a connection to Azure Cosmos DB from within Azure Databricks using the Azure Cosmos DB connector. The following Python code has a placeholder for the master key of the Azure Cosmos DB instance and assumes that NIA has an Azure Cosmos DB instance that is called **NIAAnalytics**, which has a collection called **flights_data**. The code saves a **flights** DataFrame (Spark DataFrame) to Azure Cosmos DB:

```
# Config to connect to Cosmos db
config = {
    "Endpoint": "https://NIAairport.documents.azure.com:443/",
    "Masterkey": "{masterKey}",
    "Database": "NIAAnalytics",
    "Collection": "flights_data",
    "Upsert": "true"


}


# Writing flights data from DataFrame to Azure Cosmos db
flightsDf.write.format("com.microsoft.azure.cosmosdb.spark").options(**config).save()
```

Azure Cosmos DB

Role in the Design

Azure Cosmos DB serves two main purposes: it stores all the application data for applications such as the Passengers Hub and Airport Brain apps, and it is also used to serve curated data that is ready for consumption by the airport staff and external stakeholders (such as passengers).

Why Azure Cosmos DB?

There are many options for storing NIA's curated data and application data. However, the NIA business intelligence team decided to choose Azure Cosmos DB for the following reasons:

- Azure Cosmos DB provides out-of-the-box turnkey global distribution, which is great for ensuring the availability and resiliency of the NIA platform. Understandably, NIA cannot afford downtime because it serves millions of passengers all year round. Thus, its new platform needs to have high availability which can be powered by Azure Cosmos DB.

- The NIA platform needs to provide data in near real time. Therefore, it is important to reduce latency. Azure Cosmos DB enables NIA to have a single-digit millisecond latency. This is also complemented by Azure Cosmos DB's impressive SLA of 99.999%.

- As mentioned before, NIA estimates its current data to be over 310 TB, with a growth rate of 15 GB per day. This does not yet include data coming from airline partners and external data sources such as weather and traffic. For this reason, the team chose Azure Cosmos DB for its elastic and unlimited scalability. Azure Cosmos DB provides NIA with the scalability it needs with the option to only pay for what is used in terms of storage and throughput.

- The airport currently has multiple internal systems to hold its current data, including SQL servers and MongoDB servers. The team wants to have greater compatibility with all these existing source systems and to enable existing applications to work with the new database without having to make any changes. Azure Cosmos DB is the perfect choice for this requirement because it provides a multi-model engine with a wire protocol-compatible API endpoint. This means that NIA applications can connect to the same Azure Cosmos DB instance using multiple drivers, such as MongoDB, SQL, and Gremlin. This simplifies development and deployment effort because it uses the same drivers' APIs, and it also reduces the total cost of ownership because of the room for knowledge transfer and the reduction of the need to rework.

- Another feature of Azure Cosmos DB that appealed to the NIA business intelligence team was the ability to do real-time operational analytics and AI on top of Cosmos DB. Azure Cosmos DB has out-of-the-box integration with Apache Spark and enables running Jupyter Notebooks to work with data in Cosmos DB directly without further integration or custom development work.

- Commercially, Azure Cosmos DB is a cost-effective option because it offers the business intelligence team the flexibility and control that is needed. The beauty of using Azure Cosmos DB is its ability to offer planet-scale functionality with the ability to control the costing model based on the storage and throughput that is needed. This means that when an update is executed on a record in Azure Cosmos DB, every user in the world can see this update within milliseconds.

- Finally, Azure Cosmos DB is a fully managed service, which means the NIA team will only need to care about the data it stores in Cosmos DB without worrying about the infrastructure. Moreover, this allows the team to start quickly and cheaply, and to scale as they start onboarding more datasets and demonstrating more business value.

Sample Implementation

One of the nice things about Azure Cosmos DB is its compatibility with many querying models and drivers. The following code snippets show how Cosmos DB can be queried using SQL or MongoDB. Both samples are written in C#:

1. The first code snippet queries records from the **passengers** table, looking up passengers with the name **Bob**. Then, it iterates through all the returned results and prints the name of the passenger to the console:

```
var sqlQuery = "SELECT * FROM P WHERE P.FirstName = 'Bob'";
Console.WriteLine("Running query: {0}\n", sqlQueryText);
var queryDefinition = new QueryDefinition(sqlQueryText);
var queryResultSetIterator = this.container
                    .GetItemQueryIterator<Passenger>(queryDefinition);

List<Passenger> passengers = new List<Passenger>();
while (queryResultSetIterator.HasMoreResults)
{
    var currentResultSet = await queryResultSetIterator.ReadNextAsync();
    foreach (Passenger p in currentResultSet)
    {
        passengers.Add(p);
        Console.WriteLine("\tRead {0}\n", p);
    }
}
```

2. The second code snippet performs a similar query, but it uses the MongoDB API. It creates **MongoClientSettings** first and then **MongoClient**, which is then used to get a reference to Azure Cosmos DB. The code assumes that the configuration settings have already been configured at this point. The code creates a reference to NIA's Azure Cosmos DB (**NIAAnalytics**) and queries **passengerCollection**:

```
var settings = new MongoClientSettings();
MongoClient client = new MongoClient(settings);

var dbName = "NIAAnalytics";
var collectionName = "Passengers";

var database = client.GetDatabase(dbName);
var passengerCollection = database.
GetCollection<Passenger>(collectionName);

passengers = passengerCollection.Find(new BsonDocument()).ToList();
```

Azure Machine Learning Services

Role in the Design

Azure Machine Learning Services is used by the NIA business intelligence team to operationalize their machine learning models. To optimize resource allocation, the team needs to build a number of machine learning models to predict the number of passengers and to create a recommendation for gate allocation. Azure Machine Learning Services gives the business intelligence team a consistent and reproducible way of generating machine learning models, while keeping track of all machine learning experiments, datasets, and machine learning training environments at the same time. This is critical for any machine learning model implementation where explainability is a basic requirement by customers and stakeholders.

Why Azure Machine Learning Services?

- Azure Machine Learning Services enables NIA to streamline and accelerate the whole machine learning life cycle, from data cleanup and feature engineering to model creation and validation. Azure Machine Learning Services makes it easy to automate many parts of the pipeline. This in turn reduces overhead, improves quality, and allows the NIA team to innovate more quickly.

- Versioning and maintaining multiple snapshots of datasets is a common practice when creating and experimenting with machine learning models. It can be a very tedious and confusing process to maintain multiple versions of the same datasets. Azure Machine Learning Services provides a full set of features that aim to help customers such as NIA tackle this challenge. Azure Machine Learning datasets enable NIA to track, version, and validate datasets with ease, as can be seen in the *Sample implementation* section.

- Part of the challenge for any advanced analytics team is finding the right algorithm to use to create a machine learning model. Not only does the NIA business intelligence team need to pick the right algorithm, but they also need to fine-tune any hyperparameters. Azure Machine Learning Services automates this whole process so that any data analyst can be a data scientist. Azure AutoML enables NIA's business intelligence team to automate the process of creating machine learning models quickly, easily, and cheaply.

- Compatibility is also another big plus of Azure Machine Learning Services. Azure Machine Learning Services integrates nicely with open source tools such as Databricks. It also enables NIA to use any machine learning frameworks (such as TensorFlow and PyTorch), while at the same time taking full advantage of Azure Machine Learning Services.

- Azure provides organizations such as NIA with all the latest breakthrough innovations in data and AI. One of these breakthroughs is the concept of abstracting computing from the actual data and its pipeline. This enables the NIA business intelligence team to write their code once and run it on any compute. This includes data transformation code and machine learning model code. The NIA team can build their machine learning model, run it locally on their development machines, and when ready, move that code to run on the cloud. This provides developers and organizations with great flexibility in terms of development and operational costs. NIA can pay only for the compute they need and only run the training of the machine learning models on the cloud when large computing resources are needed.

- NIA's CIO is a strong believer of DevOps and the benefits it brings to an organization. Support for DevOps processes was a major factor in deciding to choose Azure Machine Learning Services. Azure Machine Learning Services has native integration with Azure DevOps, which allows NIA to create and deploy machine learning models with ease.

- Security, reproducibility, and governance are all significant concerns for any advanced analytics team. Microsoft Azure addresses all these nicely and elegantly through native integration with other Azure services that are all battle-tested for enterprises. Azure Machine Learning Services offers out-of-the-box integration with Azure AD and Azure Monitor. Moreover, using Azure Resource Manager templates and Azure Blueprints, organizations such as NIA can enforce proper governance and standards.

Sample Implementation

Azure Machine Learning Services makes it easy to version, track, and work with multiple versions of a dataset for machine learning purposes. The following code snippet first creates a data store to tell Azure Machine Learning Services where it should store the data:

```
# creating a ref to Azure ML Service Workspace
import azureml.core
from azureml.core import Workspace, Datastore
ws = Workspace.from_config()


# Registering Azure Blob container as the datastore
datastore = Datastore.register_azure_blob_container(workspace=ws, datastore_
name='NIA_airport_datastore',
container_name='NIA_Analytics',
account_name={storageAccount},
account_key={storageAccountKey},
create_if_not_exists=True)


# get named datastore (if exist)
datastore = Datastore.get(ws, datastore_name='NIA_airport_datastore')
```

The preceding code snippet written in Python first creates an Azure Machine Learning Services workspace from an existing configuration file. The code then creates a datastore by registering an Azure Blob container as the data store. The sample names the datastore **NIA_airport_datastore** and has placeholders for the Azure Storage account name and key. Finally, the sample creates a reference to a datastore that already exists by using its name.

The following code snippet registers a new dataset and provide a name, a description, and a tag to make it easier to find this dataset in the future:

```
passengers_ds = passengers_ds.register(workspace =ws,name='passengers_
dataset',description = 'passengers personal data and address',tags =
{'year': '2019'})
```

The following code snippet retrieves an existing dataset by name and/or version ID. This is very useful when we have multiple versions of the same dataset:

```
#get Passengers dataset by name

passengers_ds = ws.datasets['passengers_dataset']


# get specific version of the passengers dataset

passengers_ds = ws.datasets['passengers_dataset']

passengers_ds_v3 = passengers_ds.get_definition(version_id = 3)
```

Azure Container Registry

Role in the Design

Azure Machine Learning Services enables the NIA business intelligence team to create their machine learning models as standard containers that can be run on any container engine, such as Docker and Kubernetes. The team uses Azure Container Registry to securely host and share these Docker containers, which hold their machine learning models.

Why Azure Container Registry?

- Azure Container Registry enables NIA to store images for all types of containers. Azure Container Registry abstracts the hosting of the images from the deployment of these images to the different deployment targets, such as Docker Swarm and Kubernetes. This enables NIA to use one container registry (ACR) to host images for all types of containers.

- Azure Container Registry builds on the functionalities of the standard container registries. For instance, Azure Container Registry integrates with Azure AD to improve security. Moreover, Azure Container Registry provides a simple way to integrate with container actions using triggers. For instance, NIA can configure a webhook to trigger Azure DevOps Services when a new image is added to Azure Container Registry.

- Azure Container Registry is fully compatible with the standard Docker Registry v2. This means that the NIA team can use the same open source Docker **command-line interface (CLI)** tools to interact with both registries (Azure Container Registry and Docker Registry v2).

- Azure Container Registry supports multi-region replication. This appeals to NIA because it helps with two things. First, it reduces network latency and cost by keeping the container registry close to the deployment targets. Second, it improves business continuity and disaster recovery since the same container registry is replicated across multiple regions.

Sample Implementation

The following code is part of the **Azure Resource Manager** (**ARM**) template that NIA uses to create the Azure Container Registry instance. It creates an Azure Container Registry (Standard tier) instance in Azure's South Africa North data center. The template also enables the Admin User account to manage the registry. The ARM template has two parameters: one parameter for the name of the registry and another parameter for the ARM API version:

```
{
    "resources": [
        {
            "name": "[parameters('registryName')]",
            "type": "Microsoft.ContainerRegistry/registries",
            "location": "South Africa North",
            "apiVersion": "[parameters('registryApiVersion')]",
            "sku": {
                "name": "Standard"
            },
            "properties": {
                "adminUserEnabled": "True"
            }
        }
    ]
}
```

Azure Kubernetes Service (AKS)

Role in the Design

Azure Kubernetes Service (AKS) is used to serve machine learning models as consumable APIs. An example of these machine learning models is a model that predicts crowd movement through the airport. Such models are trained by the team using historical data in Azure Databricks. Then, using Azure Machine Learning Services, the model is pushed as a Docker image. AKS runs these models and other apps, such as Passenger Hub. Moreover, AKS helps manage the service discovery of these apps, provides auto-scaling mechanisms, and facilitates self-healing policies for handling errors and failures.

Why AKS?

- Managing a cluster of computers is a hard task, and it is even harder to manage and configure a Kubernetes cluster. That is because Kubernetes has many moving parts and requires lots of configuration. AKS simplifies this by offering a managed cluster. This means Microsoft Azure manages the master nodes and the NIA team only needs to configure and use the slave nodes for deploying their workloads. This reduces the overhead for NIA significantly.

- Using concepts such as **virtual node** and **virtual kubelet**, AKS allows NIA to provision additional capacity elastically at any time. This is important for NIA because it is very hard to predict the load and the capacity needed, and therefore it is important to have this elastic provisioning when needed.

- The native integration and support for AKS in Azure DevOps is another advantage of AKS. This simplifies configuring and automating deployments of NIA workloads into AKS. AKS also has native integration with services such as Azure Monitor and Azure Key Vault.

- The NIA team can improve and speed up the end-to-end development experience using the Visual Studio Code's support for AKS.

- Besides the native integration with other Azure services, AKS integrates nicely with Azure Active Directory. This means that NIA can improve security by taking advantage of this integration. Furthermore, NIA can use Azure Policy to enforce governance across the whole organization.

- Azure provides great support for open source tools such as Kubernetes, not only in the cloud but also on the edge. The NIA team understands that there are scenarios where pushing computing to the edge might be the best option. An example of this is their plan to push machine learning models close to traffic monitoring cameras to trigger alerts when a safety event occurs. Microsoft Azure has good support for running Kubernetes on Azure IoT Edge for such scenarios. Therefore, using AKS will be a good option for future plans to push machine learning models to the edge using Kubernetes with Azure IoT Edge.

Sample Implementation

The following code snippet is part of NIA's Azure DevOps Services pipeline that deploys the new Airport Brain web application. The code takes advantage of Azure DevOps' support for Kubernetes by using the **KubernetesManifest** task type. The task deploys the Docker image at **nia/aiportbrain:lastest** to the pre-configured AKS by using **NIAairport_AksServcieConnection**. The following code has a placeholder for **imagePullSecret**, which is used as the authentication mechanism to pull images from Azure Container Registry to the deployment target (AKS):

```
steps:
- task: "KubernetesManifest@0"
  displayName: "Deploy AirportBrain to K8s"
  inputs:
    action: deploy
    kubernetesServiceConnection: "NIAairport_AksServiceConnection"
    namespace: "airportbrain"
    manifests: "manifests/deployment.yml"
    containers: 'nia/airportBrain:latest'
    imagePullSecrets: |
      $(imagePullSecret)
```

Power BI

Role in the Design

Part of Zara's strategy for NIA's reporting is to have Power BI as the visualization tool within NIA. Power BI can be used to generate reports and dashboards and for self-service purposes. The BI team is hoping to also take advantage of Power BI's ability to be embedded into other web apps to reuse Power BI visualizations inside other new apps, such as Passenger Hub.

Why Power BI?

Besides all the benefits of Power BI that were mentioned in *Use case 1*, Power BI reports and dashboards can be embedded into other web applications. The NIA business intelligence team wants to take advantage of the simplicity and power of Power BI's visuals to build the dashboards for the Passenger Hub and Airport Brain apps. To do this, the team can take advantage of the Power BI service's web embedding feature. Using this feature, the NIA business intelligence team can build and ship reports quickly and easily, while at the same time serving them securely through NIA's new web applications.

Sample Implementation

In Power BI, you can embed any Power BI report inside any web page. From the **File** menu, select the **Web Publish** option. This creates a dialog box that allows you to generate an embed code:

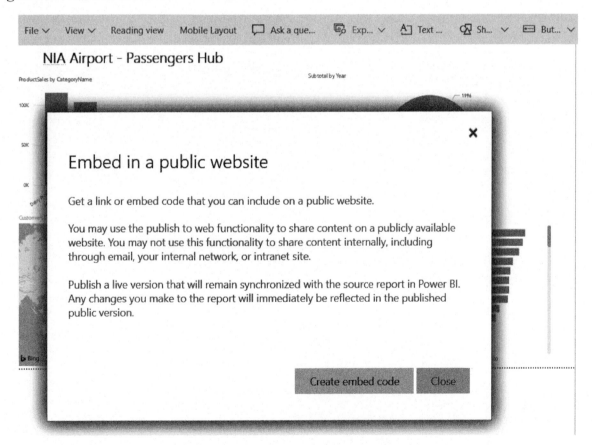

Figure 5.7: Creating an embed code

Clicking on the **Create embed code** button will generate an `iFrame` code that can be used on any HTML web page. The next dialog box allows the NIA team members to configure the properties of the `iFrame` code, such as the **width** and **height**. Then using the `iFrame` code, the report can be embedded into any web application:

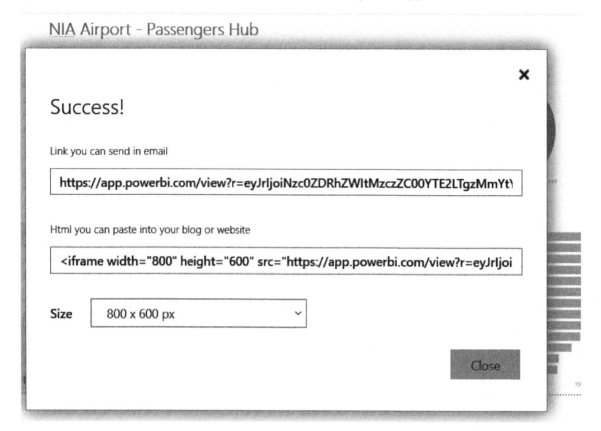

Figure 5.8: Configuring the iFrame properties

Supporting Services

NIA wants to ensure that the new solution is secure and scalable and has a good level of monitoring and support. Azure has many services that enable organizations such as NIA to secure, scale, and monitor their solutions. This includes all the services listed in *Use case 1*, such as Azure DevOps, Azure Key Vault, and Azure Monitor.

Insights and Actions

Azure helped NIA draw meaningful insights after analysis and deploy necessary measures as discussed in the following sections.

Reducing Flight Delays by 17% Using Predictive Analytics

Description: While performing initial data discovery and exploration, the NIA business intelligence team found that inefficient gate assignment was a major contributor to flight delays. Flight delays have a snowball effect because a delay in one flight can impact the next flight and the one after that. There is also the negative passenger experience that it produces. Currently, the assignment of gates at NIA is based on the capacity of their waiting area and the maximum capacity of the airplanes. This assumes that all flights are full, which is not necessarily true.

Combining weather data, city traffic data, historical flight delay data, and other sources allowed the business intelligence team to produce a better recommendation engine for gate assignment. The new recommendation engine, which was built using machine learning, looks at contextual (weather and traffic) data and historical data to estimate the number of passengers on a given flight and assign a gate accordingly. During initial modeling and validation, the team found that deploying such a recommendation engine in the Airport Brain app can reduce flight delays by 17%.

Estimated Business Value: $14.7M/year

Key Data Sources: Airlines flight data, airport data (layout and gates), weather data, city traffic data, school calendars, and public holiday calendar.

Actions: The NIA business intelligence team deployed the solution using the architecture shown in *Figure* 5.6. As a result of this solution, the airport management now has a new tool as part of the new portal (**Airport Brain**) to provide real-time recommendations for assigning gates. This improves efficiency and reduces operational overhead by excluding assumptions in planning and introducing operational decisions that are made based on facts and science.

Data Pipeline: The simplified data pipeline for this initiative is shown in *Figure* 5.9:

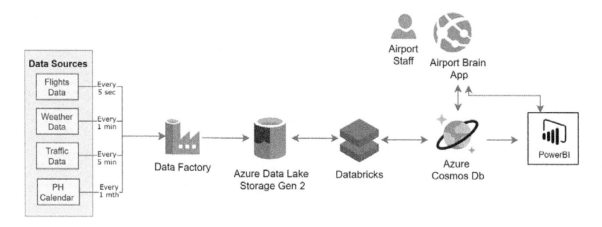

Figure 5.9: Data pipeline for initiative 1

Reducing Congestion and Improving Retail Using Smart Visualization

Description: Another encouraging discovery that the NIA business intelligence team found was the correlation between passengers' arrival time by car and long queues. The team found that when many passengers arrive at the airport more than 4 hours before their flight departure time, long queues and overcrowding became an issue. This can be attributed to the fact that the airport management team did not expect/plan for these passengers to be there at this time, which caused the long queues and congestion. Another explanation that one of the senior managers at the airport had was the fact that these early-arriving passengers were going directly to the gate and not to other facilities of the airport.

Therefore, the team decided to address this issue by directing these early-arriving passengers to other facilities of the airport, such as the duty-free area, the cinema, and the rest areas. Based on initial testing, the team estimates that this can increase retail opportunities by 11% while at the same time reduce overcrowding at the airport gates by approximately 15%.

Estimated Business Value: $9.3M/year

Key Data Sources: Airline flight data, airport data (layout and gates), weather data, passenger info, airport retail data, and public holiday calendar.

Actions: Based on these findings, the team created new dashboards in the Passenger Hub app. When passengers arrive early and scan their ID, the Passenger Hub app shows them their flight details and guides them to rest areas, duty-free shops, and the airport cinema. The team also used real-time traffic monitoring data to create large signs to be used on large screens across the airport so that users can see them without even scanning.

Data Pipeline: The simplified data pipeline for this initiative is as shown in *Figure 5.10*:

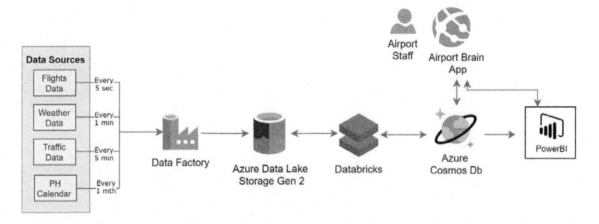

Figure 5.10: Data pipeline for initiative 2

Conclusion

Airports have complex operations and procedures, and they run around the clock. Thus, even making small improvements can provide great savings to the airport and can improve safety and customer satisfaction.

In the previous few pages, you have considered a practical example of a large airport. Although the names are fictitious, many of the numbers discussed here are based on an actual use case that the author was involved in. You have seen how advanced analytics can be used to improve efficiency and save an organization millions of dollars. Data can be used not only to help airports save on their operational costs, but also to create a competitive advantage.

You have also looked at how a data-driven solution can be implemented using Azure and why Azure is the perfect platform for running such workloads. Azure is affordable, secure, and provides organizations with the ability to be agile and scalable.

6
Conclusion

Throughout this book, you studied a number of technologies that Azure offers for cloud analytics. This journey helped you explore the comprehensive set of Azure services to ingest, store, and analyze data from various data sources such as database tables, files, streaming and other data types.

This final chapter will focus on the Modern Data Warehouse Life Cycle to bring all of these Azure services and concepts together and highlight each of their benefits. It will also explain how several of these services are adopted by organizations across the globe.

Azure Modern Data Warehouse Life Cycle

The Modern Data Warehouse Life Cycle provides you with a robust foundation for all enterprise analytics. This life cycle empowers you to perform any analytics (ranging from SQL queries to advanced Machine Learning), without having to compromise on the fidelity of your data or over-provisioning compute resources which could otherwise be under-utilized.

The Modern Data Warehouse Life Cycle consists of five steps:

1. Ingesting the data

2. Storing the data

3. Preparing and Training the data

4. Modeling and Serving the results

5. Visualization

As the variety of data, in terms of structure and complexity, continues to grow and the type of analytics you want to perform evolves, data scientists and engineers need capabilities that can meet these changing requirements. This is where the Azure Modern Data Warehouse Life Cycle comes in. Azure has the technology to meet the requirements whether you are working with structured tabular data, or dealing with large or complex unstructured big data coming from devices, services, and applications.

To bring all the Azure services and concepts together, this chapter will revisit each of the five processes in the Modern Data Warehouse Life Cycle.

Ingesting the Data

Earlier, you learned that implementing the modern data warehouse solution begins with ingesting the data in Azure. You first connect disparate datasets from multiple sources and ingest them into Azure. Data can come from RDBMS tables containing customer information such as names, address, phone numbers and credit card details. It can also be semi-structured coming from social media platforms such as Twitter feeds, or unstructured coming from IoT sensors. Your data can originate in your on-premises data center, in cloud services or both.

Azure allows you to ingest data using robust services for batch ingestion or real-time ingestion so you can capture events as they are being generated from your services and devices. This section will discuss the tools and services used for this step.

Azure Data Factory

Azure Data Factory is the primary service for batch ingestion of data. It is a fully managed ingestion, orchestration, and scheduling service which enables data integration at scale. Azure Data Factory helps you create end-to-end data pipelines that can ingest data from different sources, process and transform such datasets, schedule and trigger event driven pipelines, and provide data visualization.

The benefit of Azure Data Factory is that it provides out-of-the-box connectors to connect to everything from other clouds (such as Amazon S3) to SaaS applications (such as Salesforce or Google AdWords) and hybrid connectivity (such as SQL, MongoDB or Oracle) that exist in your on-premises data centers. Currently, Azure Data factory integrates with over 80 natively built and maintenance-free connectors at no added cost.

For example, LUMEDX (a California based organization), provides cardiologists with cardiovascular information systems for patient healthcare. It uses Azure Data Factory to ingest structured and unstructured data from multiple sources and to process this data to derive insights and deploy data pipelines at rapid speeds. This enables healthcare organizations to offer better solutions to its patients in a timely manner.

Azure Import/Export Service

If you have massive volumes of data that you want to ingest into Azure, you can consider the Azure Import/Export service. Import/Export Service uses the **WAImportExport** command-line tool that uses BitLocker to encrypt the data on the hard drive that you intend to ship to an Azure data center. Organizations can benefit from the Azure Import/Export Service in the following cases:

- When large amounts of data are to be migrated to Azure in a fast and cost-effective way.

- When large amounts of data are to be recovered from the cloud and delivered to an on-premises location.

- When on-premises data needs to be backed-up and stored in the cloud.

Azure Data Migration Service

If you have structured data, the Azure Data Migration Service allows you to ingest it by migrating it from on-premises structure databases into Azure, while maintaining the same relational structures used by your current applications. The benefit of this approach is that you can minimize changes to your existing data structure as you migrate the data to Azure.

Azure Event Hubs

Azure Event Hubs offers big data streaming and real-time event ingestion with dynamic scaling capabilities. The benefit of Azure Event Hubs is its ability to handle millions of events per second which enables large-scale telemetry and event ingestion with durable buffering and low latency from millions of devices and events.

For example, Pizza Express, a UK based company, uses Azure Event Hubs along with Azure Data Factory to track customer activity by ingesting data from multiple sources and in different formats. This helps them understand customer preferences and come up with various strategies for customer retention.

Azure IoT Hub

Azure IoT Hub is a device-to-cloud telemetry data service for tracking and understanding the state of your devices and assets. It is a managed and secure service used for bi-directional communication between IoT devices and Azure.

For example, Bridgestone (one of the world's leading tire manufacturers), developed a solution called Tirematics using Azure services. Tirematics sends data from tire sensors to Azure, which helps engineers detect early signs of tire issues such as temperature and pressure abnormalities. The Tirematics solution uses Azure IoT Hub, which receives data from tire sensors and stores it in the data lake. Stream Analytics is then used to analyze this data and detect abnormalities.

Azure CLI

The **Azure command line interface** (**CLI**) is a cross-platform command-line environment for managing Azure resources. The benefits of Azure CLI is that you can write scripts to programmatically target and ingest multiple data formats into Azure.

Azure SDK

Another way to ingest data into Azure is by using the **Azure Software Development Kit** (**SDK**). The benefit of Azure SDK is that it allows developers to write custom applications to ingest various data formats into Azure.

All of these tools and services help you ingest your data. Next, you will need to decide how you want to store the ingested data.

Storing the Data

Storing the ingested data is the second step in the modern data warehouse Life Cycle. The following section will discuss the tools and services used for this step.

Azure Blob Storage

Azure Blob Storage can store massive datasets (including videos, images, and more), irrespective of their structure, and keep it ready for analysis. The benefit of Azure Blob Storage is that it is simple to provision and can handle data available in various formats and structures.

Azure Data Lake Storage Gen2

You have seen that Azure Data Lake Storage Gen2 is a cost-efficient, analytics-optimized storage platform. It is built on top of Azure Blob Storage and is entirely independent of any compute engines. This provides a platform to accumulate and organize any form of data that will then fuel the analytics engines. The benefit of using Azure Data Lake Storage Gen2 is that, since storage is separated from compute, the compute can be tailored independently to minimize costs.

Piraeus Bank (one of Greece's largest financial institutions) uses Microsoft Azure to derive insights in order to understand customer performance and their usage and create new management KPIs using the data extracted from Azure Data Lake and Azure Data Factory.

Azure SQL Database

You can use Azure SQL Database for operational and transactional data in structured or relational form. Azure SQL Database works like the on-premises Microsoft SQL Server, but as an Azure service. The benefit of Azure SQL Database is that you do not have to worry about managing or scaling your host infrastructure. If you prefer, you can also host your existing database apps in Windows or Linux-based virtual machines on Azure.

The Barcelona Smart City Project collects and analyzes a variety of data from various systems and public sources, such as GPS signals, software log files and social media. This allows them to gain insights into government effectiveness and provide better services to citizens by improving collaboration between the government, its people, and businesses. They use Azure SQL Database to store a variety of data, such as election results, public facilities, population data, city calendars, contractor profiles, and so on. They further use this data to create a dashboard to provide near-real-time insights of around 120 KPIs to citizens. These KPIs provide information about various points (such as public bike usage, economy, population demographics, bus routes used by citizens, etc.).

Azure Synapse Analytics

For analytical data that has been aggregated over the years, Azure Synapse Analytics provides an elastic petabyte-scale service which lets you dynamically scale your data, either on-premises or in Azure. It works seamlessly with Azure Data Factory, Azure Machine Learning, HDInsight, and Power BI. Through its parallel and distributed processing architecture, Azure Synapse Analytics is capable of immense compute power. The scalable nature of Azure Synapse Analytics can handle the most complex analytical workload requirements.

Komatsu is one of the world's leading construction machinery companies. It developed a smart factory platform known as KOM-MICS to visualize and optimize plant operating conditions by collecting data through tools and robots. Komatsu has used Azure since January 2017 to collect and store the data generated by KOM-MICS. Komatsu uses Azure SQL Database to manage the master data collected by each KOM-MICS system and then aggregates all this data using the Azure Synapse Analytics. This data is then visualized using Power BI.

Azure Cosmos DB

As mentioned in *Chapter 5, Business Use Cases,* Azure Cosmos DB provides turnkey globally distributed NoSQL DB service which can be considered when dealing with schema-agnostic data. It allows you to use key/value tables, graph, and document data together with multiple consistency levels to cater to your application requirements. It provides minimum latency, high availability, and unlimited scalability. Data replication on a global level allows users to be as close to the data as possible for the most optimal data access speed worldwide. Core to Azure Cosmos DB is the concept of consistency models, where you can select up to five consistency models for your application to ensure data consistency and reliable performance, as follows:

- strong consistency
- bounded staleness
- session
- consistent prefix
- eventual consistency

Azure Cosmos DB automatically indexes all the data for you regardless of which model you choose. You can scale storage and throughput globally across Azure regions independently and elastically. This provides predictable throughput, consistency, and high availability. It is ideal for scenarios where you are working with globally distributed mission critical applications, as well as retail e-commerce, IoT, mobile, and gaming applications.

Archive 360 is an organization that helps its customers migrate and manage large amounts of data from legacy on-premises systems to the cloud. They use Cosmos DB to deal with different data types and help customers organize, classify, and manage their data.

Preparing and Training the Data

After ingesting and storing your data, you need a method to transform the data to fit your purpose. This is where scalable compute engines come in.

You can prepare and train your data and data stores to derive insights, and create predictive and prescriptive models on your data using Machine Learning and deep learning techniques.

This next section will serve as a quick recap of the services covered in this book.

Azure Databricks

Azure Databricks, an Apache Spark-based analytics cluster service, offers the best of Spark with collaborative notebooks and enterprise features. This powerful tool can perform complex transformations at scale. It integrates with Azure Active Directory and native connectors to bring in other Azure data services. Here are some examples of Azure Databricks data connectors:

- Azure SQL Database
- Azure Synapse Analytics
- Azure HDInsight (HDFS)
- SQL Server Database
- SQL Server Analysis Services Database
- MySQL Database
- Oracle Database
- Access Database
- Excel
- Text/CSV
- XML
- JSON
- File folder
- PostgreSQL Database
- Sybase Database
- Tera Database

For a big data pipeline, you can ingest the data (structured or unstructured) into Azure through Azure Data Factory in batches, or streamed near real-time using IoT Hub, Event Hub, or Kafta. For long-term persistent storage, you can store the data in Azure Data Lake Storage or Azure Blob Storage. Azure Databricks then reads the data and produces breakthrough insights using Spark. The benefit of Azure Databricks is that it is an excellent platform for producing predictive models with data science.

Zeiss, a leading manufacturer of high-end optical systems, were finding it difficult to scale their infrastructure to analyze massive volumes of unstructured data. Azure Databricks provided them with a unified analytics platform that solved their scaling issues and offered a fully managed, highly scalable, unified service. Azure Databricks allowed Zeiss to combine batch data, along with unstructured IoT data, and simplify the data engineering process.

Azure Stream Analytics

Azure Stream Analytics uses a powerful event processing engine that analyzes patterns and relationships from the real-time data captured from devices, sensors, and more. Together with Azure Event Hubs, Azure Stream Analytics enables you to ingest millions of events and detect anomalies, power dashboards, find patterns, or automate event-driven tasks using a SQL-like language in real-time.

To return to a previous example, Piraeus Bank (the Greek financial institution), is able to monitor user experience and the online customer journey with Azure Stream Analytics and Power BI.

Azure Cognitive Services

Azure Cognitive Services allow developers to easily add cognitive features into their applications through a set of high level pre-built AI services for vision, speech, text, language, knowledge, and search. The benefit of using Azure Cognitive Services is that we can incorporate image recognition and text translations as part of our data analytics process.

For example, IndiaLends (a digital lending and borrowing marketplace), uses analytics algorithms to connect India's leading banks with millions of borrowers. They use Azure Cognitive Services for tasks such as text processing, image processing, and sentiment analysis for better customer query resolution.

Azure Machine Learning

For advanced analytics, Azure Machine Learning and Microsoft Machine Learning Server provide you the infrastructure and tools to analyze data, create high-quality data models, and to train and orchestrate Machine Learning as you build intelligent apps and services. The benefit of using Azure Machine Learning is that it delivers the predictive intelligence that businesses need to stay competitive.

British Petroleum use AI and Microsoft Machine Learning algorithms to predict the amount of hydrocarbons that can be extracted from potential oil and natural gas reservoirs. This forecasting initially required manual analysis of almost 200 different properties of the reservoir. A three-stage process of choosing the right variables, building the algorithm, and enhancing the model performance by adjusting model parameters, helps BP simplify the process and build a model that takes into consideration all possible scenarios.

Modeling and Serving the Results

Following the preparation and training step, you have analyzed and derived insights from your data. The next step is to serve the enriched data to your users.

The best destination for all of these analyzed data is Azure Synapse Analytics. Azure Synapse Analytics enables you to combine historical trends with new insights into one version of data for your organization. It is also extensible and flexible with its ability to seamlessly connect to analytics tools and services, as well as integrating with business intelligence tools.

Visualization and More

Azure Analysis Services and Power BI provide powerful options to find and share data insights. While Azure Synapse Analytics is the engine that powers these insights, Power BI is a visualization tool which empowers users to analyze the data for themselves.

In addition, you can also populate data from your insights into operational data stores like Azure SQL Database and Azure Cosmos DB to enhance the custom web and application experiences.

You can even push data directly to your apps with Azure platform tools for developers, including Visual Studio, Azure Machine Learning Studio, or custom serverless apps and services using Azure Functions.

To secure your data access, you can ensure that users are authenticated by Azure Active Directory, and that only the intended groups of users are allowed to consume the data based on your specifications.

Summary

Throughout this book, you have seen the different stages involved in performing data analytics on the cloud. The sample implementations and use cases demonstrate how real organizations have used Azure technologies in different sectors for making the most out of data, giving you an idea of how you can leverage this powerful technology to help your own business.

The cloud model for Modern Data Warehousing is not only flexible and scalable, but it is also cost effective due to its unique elastic properties. Analytics workloads are one scenario where the elasticity truly shines.

Now that you have reached the end of this book, you are armed with the knowledge of the Modern Data Warehouse and all the services and tools you need to build your own complete data analytical solution. The best way to begin is to start small, by integrating some of the technologies this book has introduced into your existing workflow, then gradually add more capabilities in the future as your needs evolve.

Learn more about the Modern Data Warehouse Lifecycle at https://packt. live/35eCCVp.

Create your free Azure subscription at https://packt.live/2Xqtj22.

Best of luck with your modern data warehouse and cloud analytics journey.

Index

About

All major keywords used in this book are captured alphabetically in this section. Each one is accompanied by the page number of where they appear.

Printed by Amazon Italia Logistica S.r.l.
Torrazza Piemonte (TO), Italy

11567402R00142